The

MARATHON
MANIACS

The World's Most
Insane Running Club

Edited by • Malcolm Anderson

42K Books

Champaign, Illinois

Library of Congress Cataloging-in-Publication Data

Anderson, Malcolm, 1961-
  The marathon maniacs : the world's most insane running club / edited by
Malcolm Anderson.
    p. cm.
  ISBN 978-0-615-56655-9 (soft cover)
  1. Marathon running. 2. Athletic clubs. I. Title.
  GV1065.A54 2012
  796.42'4--dc23

                          2011047000

ISBN: 978-0-615-56655-9
Copyright © 2012 by The Marathon Maniacs®

Marathon Maniacs is a registered trademark owned by the Marathon Maniacs Cor-
poration, Tacoma, Washington.

Published by 42K Books, a division of 42K(+) Press, Inc.
Printed in the United States of America.

Questions regarding the content of this book should be addressed to
Tony Phillippi
tony@marathonmaniacs.com

Cover photo: The founders of the Marathon Maniacs—from left to right, Tony Phil-
    lippi, Steve Yee, and Chris Warren—at the start line of the Tacoma Narrows Half
    Marathon, Tacoma Narrows Airport, August 2011.
Editor and project manager: Jan Colarusso Seeley
Cover photo: Matt Hagen
Cover and interior design and layout: Judy Henderson
Copyeditor: Dick Lipsey
Proofreader: Ray Vallese
Printed by: Premier Print Group

Marathon Maniac Insights

"I didn't know that becoming a Maniac would change my life."
—Yolanda Holder

"Marathoning gives me joy these days, as I go at my own slow pace and breathe patiently into every step."—Cami Ostman

"Being a marathoner has helped shape my entire well-being. The marathon has given me the tools to be a better person and has given me the desire to succeed in any endeavor I attempt."—Ed Loy

"I am in enormous awe of the feats of the people in this club. Many have been inspiring."—Don Kienz

"The Marathon Maniacs community (and the feeling of accomplishment) made me understand the purpose of running."—Kelsey Swift

"The most satisfying thing to me about running is how life affirming it can be, with the sense of community shared among its participants."
—Joe "Moonie" Arcilla

"Running has become very important to my physical and mental well-being, and being a Marathon Maniac has given me a way to focus on running. Having that singlet on at races helps open many conversations. The friends I've met in the club and the stories I've heard have been very inspirational."—Ken Briggs

"Running a marathon tests our endurance, plays games with our minds, and pushes our bodies beyond what we thought possible. It turns out that cancer treatment follows a similar pattern. And now, crossing the finish line has a whole new meaning to me."—Kim Williamson

"If you are not a Maniac yet, I strongly encourage you to join this club. It is the greatest!"—Marie Zornes

"Everyone in my family and most of the folks at work think I am completely crazy. I reassure them that I am *not* crazy; I am just a confirmed Marathon Maniac!"—Marsha White

"While many of those I speak with cannot see themselves running a marathon, I see an opportunity to use this mantra: *hope, strength, determination, courage.* Let it take you places you never thought possible."—Megan Ross Hope

"You can't really separate your own determination from the love and support you receive from others—they're both essential. Being a Marathon Maniac helped me to heal."—Paul C. David

"It has been a good day of running—no injuries, no chafing, no blisters, no medical attention required. I had only one more obstacle: getting out of the car when I got home."—Mike Kuhlmann

"Becoming a Maniac was a wonderful experience. It continues to be. The encouragement from all those yellow-singlet-clad racers at marathons since 2007 has been an inspiration to me in every marathon since."—Rob Roy Smith

"Who would get married on a Wednesday night so as not to interfere with the groom's weekend races? The answer seems logical that it must be someone with Marathon Maniac tendencies."—Lenore Dolphin

"Running really does give you the confidence to go for it, no matter what 'it' is."—Pam Medhurst

"Every time I see a Maniac, I get an extra burst of encouragement through our shared camaraderie!"— Pamela Brulotte

"We rounded the final corner, and as we heard the crowd roar, I could no longer hold back the emotion, and neither could my dad. I grabbed my father's hand and hoisted it in the air. We had done it; we had completed the marathon. We had remained best friends, and in that moment we embodied everything that truly is a father-and-son story."—Stephen Bucken

"I'm compelled to share my success story with others. I want to help people who are going through what I went through. I want to give them inspiration and make them come to a realization that life is what we make of it."—Rosemarie Hernandez

"The gift is not found in the finisher's shirt or in the medal hanging around your neck. The gift is found in learning about yourself."—Cheri Fiorucci

Table of Contents

Acknowledgments

I'd like to thank *Marathon & Beyond* publisher Jan Seeley and her production team (Judy Henderson, Dick Lipsey, and Ray Vallese)—who made the book "the book"—for their energy, encouragement, enthusiasm, and expertise. I would also like to say thanks to Tony Phillippi, Chris Warren, and Steve Yee for their commitment to making the book happen and for asking me to be involved. Like everyone else, we Marathon Maniacs are born to run, but maybe it's not so much that we *can* run, it's that running gives us so much of everything that makes our lives simply more enjoyable. So I would like to thank, in large neon lights, all the contributors to the book who were so responsive and encouraging as the book went from conception to publication. I've had the pleasure of emailing and talking with a number of Maniacs, and it's had the effect of making me want to run more and meet more members of the world's most insane running club.

Introduction

by • Malcolm Anderson • Steven Yee • Chris Warren and • Tony Phillippi

This book is a compilation of dozens of stories by Marathon Maniac club members. They are thoughtful, entertaining, instructive, endearing, sometimes comical, and most often immensely inspirational. We also know that they are just the tip of the iceberg when it comes to the experiences of Marathon Maniacs.

When I (Malcolm) first started running marathons, I was inwardly focused. I wanted to run the best I could. I wanted to beat my personal best, eat and drink the right things, and be in peak physical condition. But what I discovered is that the world of distance running is much more than that. It's about the total marathon experience, and an integral part of that experience is meeting fellow runners who share the same passion—they are the friends that you make along the way.

In the distance-running world, you bond very quickly with many people. Run for two to four hours with a complete stranger, and you find yourself not only sharing the experience of the run itself but also sharing stories that will stay with you for years. Some of my closest friends are other runners whom I've met running. We learn about other people, we learn about other places, and we learn about ourselves. Sometimes we'll share feelings with another runner that we wouldn't share with our friends and family.

Why is that? There is something extremely addictive about running long distances.

We keep coming back to run and to experience more and more races. People are catching on that it's a great lifestyle. The number of marathon finishers each year continues to grow, and it doesn't look like this trend will reverse itself anytime soon. The club, the Marathon Maniacs, is a perfect place for people like ourselves who are passionate about distance running.

As well as sharing experiences—stories—with runners at race events, the club has chosen another route and has decided to publish a book that brings Maniac stories to a larger audience. In 2009, the founding Maniacs—Steve,

Tony, and Chris—felt it was time for Maniac stories to be shared with the world and invited club members to send their stories for this book.

The response was overwhelming. Whether you are a Maniac, a non-Maniac runner, or a nonrunner, we hope that you will find these stories to be a celebration and a reflection of the human condition. The contributors could have written a lot more, and in many cases we found upon reading their stories that we would have liked much more information. But the book would have been enormous, a 100-miler. Our intent has been to uncover the diversity of the Maniac running experiences, which is why there are dozens of stories instead of just a few.

Not only are the stories diverse, but so too are the contributors. It's proof again that this club is unique; it is the membership that makes it unique. We share a passion for running long distances and a passion for everything that those experiences provide. The Marathon Maniacs club is a testament to the fact that we are inherently social animals, born to run, as they say. It's the social connectedness that brings us back to the start line, the close friends and family we run with or for, the friends we have yet to meet on the course, and the other Maniacs we see as we put one foot in front of the other. It has been an absolute pleasure and a privilege to read the stories of these Maniacs in the pages that follow. We hope that you will feel the same.

For more information about the criteria for joining the Marathon Maniacs, see pages 215–216.

The Marathon Maniacs website is *www.marathonmaniacs.com*.

The Founding of the Marathon Maniacs

by • Steven Yee (MM #1) with • Chris Warren (MM #2)
and • Tony Phillippi (MM #3)

Are you addicted to running marathons? Do you think about what marathon you will be running next, even before you start the one you're currently training for? Do you plan your vacations around marathons? Have you run marathons on consecutive weekends or back-to-back days? If you answered yes to all of the above questions, you just might consider joining an exclusive club. Tony Phillippi, Chris Warren, and I have developed an infectious enthusiasm for marathon madness.

The birth of the Marathon Maniacs

It all began rather innocently. I had planned on flying to Indonesia in April 2003 to participate in the Bali Marathon with marathon traveling companions Sue Fauerbach (MM #7) and Tonee Bertalan. In 2002, we had a wonderful time in China, culminating in the running of the tough Great Wall Marathon. The thirst for more international marathons was in our blood. However, the lack of participants from the United States forced the cancellation of the Bali tour in late February, no doubt sparked by the terrorist bombing in late 2002 and the uncertainty regarding safe international travel. My attention then turned to Boston. Chris and Tony had signed up and had a room reserved, so the only caveat was whether Boston had reached its capacity. It hadn't, and I was grateful for the opportunity to change plans on such short notice.

After completing three marathons in three weeks in April (Yakima, Whidbey Island, and Boston) without too much difficulty, I sought out a further challenge. Scanning the marathon schedule, I saw that the months of May and June provided that challenge. Starting with Coeur D'Alene and following with San Diego Rock 'n' Roll, San Juan Island, and North Olympic Discovery would give me four marathons in four weeks. Tony and Chris also drove to Coeur D'Alene to participate in the marathon. After the race, we had lunch with Terry Watanabe (MM #4 from Spokane), a fellow member of the Northwest Dead Runners Society (an e-mail running chat room). As we were discussing our future race plans and mentioning all the marathons we were going to participate in, she blurted out, "You guys are a bunch of marathon maniacs"—hence the name. A club was formed, a website was created by Tony (*www.marathonmaniacs.com*), and members were recruited, including ultramaniacs. You may recognize some of the other names in the club that have fulfilled the criteria for membership in what we termed "the Insane Asylum." In fact, some of these members have graced the covers of *Northwest Runner* (for example, Mel Preedy and Doug MacLean). Thank goodness that there are others out there who think like us!

The story behind the Maniac

As the whole Maniac idea was coming together, we thought we needed an icon to make us look as distinctive as our club. We got together with running buddy Mark Ariyoshi, a graphic designer who worked with Tony. Mark suggested that we incorporate characteristics of the three founding Maniacs into an animated character that would represent a true Marathon Maniac. Everyone agreed, and Mark was soon soliciting ideas from each of us during our noontime runs. His first goal was to make the guy look like a maniac; that's where the bulging eyes and tongue hanging out of Main Maniac come in. Chris had a tendency to swing his right arm out while running; that's why the right arm is placed where it is. Tony's first website and his personalized license plate are PF FLYER, so this was written on the side of the shorts. Tony says before every race, "Let's burn some rubber," so smoke was added behind the shoes. Also, Tony has a huge battle raging to break three hours in the marathon; that's why the watch reads "2:59:59." Tony and I frequently teased Chris about a comment by a member of the Dead Runners Society, "the dazzling smile of Chris Warren," which explains the gleam of the tooth. I always wear a Timex GPS watch while doing training runs; that is what's on the left arm going "beep, beep, beep." (Remember that this story was written many moons ago, and I have since upgraded to the Garmin 310.)

Now to answer the question that everyone really wants to know: What's up with the cat on the head? Originally, when we were making out the criteria for Maniac membership, we couldn't agree on what made a Maniac. At one point in the conversation, I said that if it was a close call, the person applying for maniacism had to have a cat! Yes, a cat! Since all three of the founding Maniacs have at least one cat, it would be the tiebreaker for inclusion in the Maniac circle. Obviously, this isn't part of the real criteria, but it adds humor to the Maniac and its story.

Now fast forward to 2011. With the current membership of well over 5,000 Maniacs, it would have been hard to believe that on that fateful day in May 2003 that the Marathon Maniacs would have grown this much and this fast. But it was not always that way. During the first year of the club's inception, a mere 30 Maniacs joined the Insane Asylum. Chris, Tony, and I had to beg runners to join the club. And there was incentive for the first 20 members, who were given free lifetime membership into the club. The second year saw a slight increase to 121 members. At that time, for the three of us, that was a monumental achievement. We were congratulating ourselves! Little did we know what the future was for the Marathon Maniacs.

The next few years saw modest growth in the Insane Asylum (member #1000 was inducted on June 18, 2008). And then came the exponential growth. Like a statistical bell curve without the decline after the apex, maniacal growth of approximately 100 members per month vaulted the membership past the 2,000 and 3,000 marks in 2009 and 2010. With more than 5,000 members, the Marathon Maniacs could very well be the largest marathon club in the world. And we say "the world" because the Maniacs range from Brazil, Australia, and the United Kingdom to Malaysia, Singapore, Japan, and South Korea, with at least a few from many European nations. All 50 states are represented as well as the majority of Canadian provinces.

What caused the sudden spurt in the growth of the Maniacs? Obviously, the economic downturn was not a factor in slowing membership growth, as it seems that people are willing to give up other things but not their participation in marathons and ultras. Could it be the increase in the number of marathons, making it easier to find events to qualify for the Insane Asylum? We think the most probable reason is the culture of the Maniacs and how proud the members are in being one. Many members have told us of the camaraderie and the many friendships they have made by being a Maniac. Certainly, sporting the Maniac gear at an event is an icebreaker.

So what's in store for the Marathon Maniacs? We don't see membership slowing down anytime soon, and there are more demands for additional gear and items for members. With the ever-increasing membership, we may need to recruit more members to help maintain the services provided by the club. And we are always looking out for deals and benefits for our members. Goals for us include additional race reunions each year and a push to become even more international. But the sky is the limit for the Marathon Maniacs, and we are all enjoying the ride.

So do you think that we can share the name "10,000 Maniacs" with the rock band when we hit that level in a few years?

How I Started Running

by • Christine Adams

A year ago, I would have never imagined where I am today. I was focusing on losing weight and thought I *hated* running. I was training for the Breast Cancer Three-Day Walk by walking some 5Ks and eventually a few half-marathons. Then the bug hit me.

I heard about a group called the Marathon Maniacs and a girl in my weight-loss group who had just become one. Then I heard of a group called the Half-Fanatics. I decided that I had to do it. I had to become a Fanatic by completing three half-marathons in three months. And I did—I became Half-Fanatic #68.

But that wasn't enough. I completed my three-day walk, 60 miles in three days, in September 2009 and decided that I would try the Portland full marathon, 26.2 miles in one day—my first marathon.

I walked most of it. My time was about seven hours. I *loved* it: the medal, the tech T, the seedling, and the rose. The feeling of accomplishment was *amazing*. I was immediately hooked.

I completed my second marathon the following month in Seattle, and I ran part of it! A week later, I traveled to Vegas to complete my third, running even more, and become official Marathon Maniac #2016. Since then I have completed my fourth in Arizona, my fifth in Tacoma, and my sixth in San Diego. The amount of support I feel from my fellow Maniacs is overwhelming; what an amazing, inspirational group of people. I have learned to love running and have cut over one hour off my marathon time. This month I will be completing my seventh full marathon in Seattle. My goal is to complete my 10th full marathon in Portland, the place I started, on 10/10/10, and then to complete my first ultra at the end of October.

Postscript: *Christine completed eight full marathons in 2010. After a short break to recover from a slight knee injury, she continued running half-marathons in 2011. She reached her goal weight, losing a total of 70 pounds. Her husband has started running half-marathons and has qualified to become a Half-Fanatic.*

Becoming
Marathon Maniacs

by • Marci Martin

My husband, Bob, and I started running in late 2004 for health reasons; actually, we started walking first. We were both about a hundred pounds overweight, with blood pressure and cholesterol problems. Bob ran his first race in February 2005, a 4.4-mile run in Aberdeen, Washington. My first race was in July 2005, the 3K at Lakefair in Olympia, Washington. As we started looking for more races close to home, we discovered there were several runs frequently held at Millersylvania State Park in Olympia, usually with distances from a 5K to a marathon.

One weekend we noticed a small group of people with yellow singlets, our first sighting of the Maniacs. At the time, I don't think either of us could imagine running 26.2 miles.

The weight came off, and our running progressed. In October 2005, Bob ran his first half-marathon in 1:50:29 and decided that he was now ready for the Seattle Marathon on Thanksgiving weekend. He finished his first marathon in 3:31:13, just missing a Boston qualifier—not that he was trying to qualify. We hadn't even thought about it.

Bob has since ran 38 marathons, 34 of which have been Boston qualifiers. Bob joined the Maniacs in May 2007. My road to the marathon was a little slower. In 2008, Bob decided he was going to run six marathons in five weeks to increase his stats. I decided that I would do a half-marathon on each of those weekends. Most of the marathons had the half-marathon option except for the one in Newport, Oregon. As I tried to occupy my time waiting for Bob to get back to the finish line, I decided that I needed to try a marathon. My first would be the following weekend at the North Olympic Discovery Marathon (NODM), which starts in Sequim and ends in Port Angeles, Washington.

The experience was awesome; the weather was perfect. I did the early start, and Bob went by me at mile 24. I finished in 5:27. With one marathon down, I had to figure out how to become a Maniac. I figured that I could do the three-marathons-in-90-days option for the bronze level. As luck would have it, there was a marathon two weeks after NODM, the Seafair Marathon in Seattle, and then the Sauvie Island Marathon in Oregon. After the Sauvie Island marathon, I became Marathon Maniac #1030 (July 2008). To date, I have completed eight marathons. 🐱

Running With the Pack

by • Beth Ramirez (aka Happy Dog)

It all began so innocently. The article stated that if I simply did as instructed, I could run a half-marathon in just three months. At that time, I could maybe run a mile, possibly even two if really pressed. I had never heard of GU, fartleks, splits, or bonking.

My plan was simple. I would run this one half-marathon just to prove to myself that I could do it. It was to be my one and only race. I was given a running program that I followed to a *t*, checking off each and every training run as the weeks went by. Suddenly, race day was upon me. It was the Orange County Half-Marathon.

On the walk back to the car after the race, I saw runners with their knees wrapped in ice, and I thought how sad that they had bad knees. The next day, it suddenly dawned on me why they had the ice packs—I could hardly walk up and down our stairs!

That race was so exhilarating that I came up with a new plan: I would run one half-marathon each month for a full year, and then I would be done. After that, I would make a quilt using all of my running shirts. The thought of a full marathon never entered my mind. It was simply impossible and at 40-something just was not going to happen.

Somewhere along the line, just before I was going to quit and start on my quilt, my neighbor Kim wanted to run with me. Then my niece Shelley decided to start running, too. My friend Lori Ann was soon inspired to run with me. Then Shelley's friend Kris joined us and brought along her friend Sherie. Alberta wasn't far behind. The plans for my quilt were now put on the back burner. At this point, there were so many of us that we joked that we had formed a pack. We called ourselves "The Dogs" and gave each other dog names. I became Happy Dog, Shelley became Mad Dog Filbey, and Kris became known as Bad Dog. Kim, the fastest of the bunch, was Rocket Dog, and Lori Ann took on the moniker Haute Dog because of her love of clothes. Alberta was soon known as Wild Dog. Our newest pack members are Tracy, aka Salty Dog, and our other Traci, who answers to Sugar Dog. We all love running with the pack and eagerly look forward to our weekly long runs together. How could I possibly consider quitting now?

Then I read about the Nike Women's Marathon in San Francisco, where a fireman in a tux awards you a Tiffany necklace as you cross the finish line. Wow! Now that was truly motivational. Maybe 26.2 miles wasn't so impossible after all! So I grabbed my running dogs—Haute Dog and Rocket Dog—and we began training in earnest. Several months later, race day arrived. It was, in no uncertain terms, the best run of my life. I ran like the wind. At the finish line, I had my fireman and my necklace. I was hooked. I was a *marathon runner.*

Not long after that, Bad Dog talked Mad Dog and me into running the New York Marathon. I had already signed up for a repeat of the Nike Women's Marathon. Problem: it was just 10 days prior to the New York Marathon, which in my mind was impossible. But since both were lotteries, I figured there was no way that I would make it into both. I mean, what are the odds, right? Well, as fate would have it, I was selected for both—two marathons, 10 days apart, back to back. Yep, you know what that means! *Marathon Maniac!* Mad Dog had already become Maniac #1675 a few months earlier and proudly wore her Maniac shirt whenever she raced. Since those two races last year, I too, am a Maniac, #1919.

Since that time, I have run six more marathons and have signed up for several more. Of course, Bad Dog Kris would not be outdone and ran her three marathons in the allotted time to gain entry to the club as well. She is Maniac #2018. Most recently, Tracy, aka Salty Dog, ran the Los Angeles Marathon (in the pouring rain), the Orange County Marathon, and the San Diego Rock 'n' Roll, making her Maniac #3982. Our pack runs by three rules, which we repeat before each and every race like a mantra: (1) have fun, (2) don't get injured, and (3) finish the race.

We're hoping that the rest of the pack joins, too. After all, we all know that it's only a matter of time . . and distance. Oh, and my quilt? Before I get to that, I have to run Chicago and Napa Valley, and how could I miss the Marine Corps Marathon, showcasing our nation's memorials? Of course, there is the Marathon Maniacs Marathon each May as well.

So my new plan? I have no plan, other than to keep on running marathons and run like the wind.

5

At the Back

by • Diana Ringquist

Those who run marathons in three or four hours (or less) are amazing individuals! However, I would argue that they really don't understand what endurance sports are all about. Do you want to talk endurance and drama? Try doing just one race at the back, in the six-plus-hours category. That is where it all really happens. This is where you find the mom who thought she would never be able to do more than a mile, the girl who lost 50 pounds and has about 100 more to go, the man who suffered a heart attack and has a second chance at life, the grandmother who mourns the death of her life mate, and the boy who was pushed into running by his mom and refuses to give up.

At the back is where the blisters are deep and large, where the human spirit is tested, where perfect strangers are suddenly close friends (and remain so for years after), and where lifetimes of "I can't" become futures of "I can!" Out of the tears, sweat, support, encouragement, praise, teasing, and conversations, people are reborn in ways that cannot be understood by those on the outside.

Could I run a marathon in the sub-five-hour group or faster? Probably. But why on earth would I want to? I would miss the transformative effects of this amazing sport.

6

Proud to Be a Sister Maniac

by • Cami Ostman

The first time I was aware of meeting a Marathon Maniac, I was just beginning to buy into an existence that included regular running as a staple of my
self-care regimen. It was 2007. Bill and I had been married for two years,
and I was weeks away from turning 40. The last few years of life had been

chaotic and revolutionary for me, with a divorce, a job change, a move to Bellingham, Washington, and now this new marriage.

Bill and I had done a marathon together in Prague in 2003 while we were still "just friends," and I was considering signing up for a second one, but only considering. At the moment, we were on vacation in Madison, Wisconsin, visiting Bill's brother. Bill had signed up for the Madison Marathon, and I tagged along to applaud him over the finish line.

When the race was over and we were milling around in the recovery area, I caught a glimpse out of the corner of my eye of a fellow in a yellow singlet I thought I recognized. Doing a double take, I nudged Bill and said, "Hey, see that guy over there? Didn't we talk to him on the bus before the Crater Lake race in Oregon?" (I had run the six-mile race.) "Doesn't he live somewhere near us?"

Bill followed my gaze and said, "Yeah, that's Terry. We saw him at the Tacoma race a couple of weeks ago, too. He's a Marathon Maniac."

"A what?" I asked.

"It's a club," Bill said. "They run marathons all over the country."

"Really?" I said. "What for?"

"Fun."

"Hmm," I pondered. "How strange."

I hadn't found my one and only marathon fun, exactly, but I had felt that the experience was profound, challenging what I thought I knew about my mental and physical limits. Still, although I was growing more and more committed to long-distance running, there wasn't much joy in it for me yet. I tucked the image of the yellow singlet into my memory for future reference.

During the next year, Bill and I traveled to Australia and, indeed, ran a marathon there in a little wine-producing town called Mudgee. In fact, we concocted a plan to run a marathon on every continent, a pretty bold decision for someone like me who had run only two 42K races in her life. I liked having the goal, enjoyed traveling, and continued to feel that running was teaching me invaluable lessons about myself, but it was hard for me, too. I was bored with myself on long runs and often irritated by the time it took to train.

Then I had my next Maniac sighting. I met Mel about halfway into the 2008 Whidbey Island Marathon. The Whidbey race is brutally hilly. I was in the midst of wondering whether I was crazy to be running it at all when

I hit a much-needed downward slope and saw Mel, 75 years old that year. I puttered up next to him and struck up a conversation. He told me that he had run a race the previous weekend and had one planned the next. If that didn't astound me enough, he then reported that he was healing from a cracked hip.

What the heck? I thought. *Who runs three marathons three weeks in a row while healing from a cracked hip? Doesn't that kill the body? Wouldn't you be exhausted?*

But as I ran with Mel, his positive attitude and joy rubbed off on me. He hadn't started marathoning until he was 50, he told me. Now he was a Maniac. He explained to me that marathon running made him feel alive and healthy, like he was really celebrating life. And there was no denying that he looked happy. *There must be something to this Maniac thing,* I said to myself.

Eventually, I ran ahead of Mel that day, but something in his attitude had really challenged me. I had been a grudging runner up to that point, chugging along and complaining the whole distance. I thought it was good for me but not necessarily something that lifted my spirits.

My complaining days were over after meeting Mel. He knew something about life that I needed to understand in my 40th year: to find joy in what you're doing, you've got to take your time, breathe deeply, and keep moving forward with a smile.

Still, I didn't think of becoming a Maniac myself until I encountered some very special female Maniacs over the next two years. At nearly every running event I attended in Bellingham, I bumped into a woman named Diana and her sister-in-law, Stacy. The two of them shone as they sailed along the racecourses we all traversed. Through the grapevine, I learned that Diana had had some serious health problems and that running had helped her heal. And Stacy was there cheering and running beside her. I was encouraged every time I saw them. For a long time, they didn't know that I was watching them, but I eventually overcame my shyness and approached them, listening as Diana told me, "In the Maniacs, it doesn't matter how fast you go, only how many races you do." This resonated with me—a back-of-the-packer who sometimes wondered whether the late-staying volunteers greeting me at the finish line were annoyed at having to wait for me.

When I finally met Marina (#1075), two years after seeing Terry in Madison, I was nearly ready to take the pledge. It was time for me to become a Maniac. Unlike the way I had encountered the other Maniacs who inspired me, I didn't meet Marina at a race. I met her online. From California, she responded to an e-mail I had sent out to as many marathon-runner lists as I could get my hands on, trying to find a few people to go to Antarctica with me. I couldn't get into the official Antarctica Marathon, and I wanted company as I tried to get permission to run unofficially on that last continent. Marina responded to my plea with fervor, and she never wavered when everyone else did, though we hit one roadblock after another. Problems with government permission and even a huge Chilean earthquake damaging our stopover airport couldn't discourage her. Marina didn't care what it took; she was going!

I'm not sure that I would have stuck with the plan on my own, but like so many other Maniacs, Marina was absolutely relentless. She had run 28 marathons in 2009, and she was determined to cross South America and Antarctica off her list before another year went by. For my part, I was so touched by her commitment to our mutual dream and awed by her love of marathon running that I woke up one morning and said to Bill, "I need to be a Maniac! These people are so enthusiastic; I have to become one of them."

"Do it," he said.

I took the easy route into the club, I must admit, running three races (the Last Chance Marathon in Bellingham, the Pigtails Ultra in Renton, and the Birch Bay Marathon) within 58 days. A little tired but a lot happy, I joined the club of people who had been inspiring me for the past few years. And I'm honored to call myself one of them.

I may never be as maniacal as Mel or Marina, but I know this much—marathoning gives me joy these days as I go at my own slow pace and breathe patiently into every step. Let this be my thanks to the Maniacs who showed me the way. You're my impetus to keep on going.

7

March-Madness Mentality

by • Caroline Burnet

When you're training for marathons and ultras, you run—a lot. Combine this fact with the laws of probability, throw in occasional bad luck (or inane stupidity), and it stands to reason that you will find yourself in a few unenviable situations.

For starters, there was the 20-mile training run on the American Tobacco Trail while visiting my parents in Apex, North Carolina. Though the lack of drinking fountains was well advertised, the trail map illustrated restrooms every few miles. This would suffice as a water source except that upon entering each of said restrooms, I was greeted by nothing more than a glorified porta-potty, complete with a proud sign lauding the plumbingless engineering marvel. Ouch.

Or there was another 20-miler in rare Atlanta subfreezing temperatures. That alone was enough to induce sufficient misery. Add in the downpour and 15-mile-per-hour winds, and the brutality of it all was spelled across the concerned faces of passing motorists . . . right as their SUVs sent three inches of standing water my way in a continuous neck-high spray assault.

But these were mere inconveniences compared with what was planned as an easy recovery eight-mile out-and-back from my condo. All was well until three miles in, when I started to feel sick—sick as in the "need to find a bathroom posthaste" variety. As a typically stubborn distance runner hell bent on not cutting any route short, I forged ahead, determined to make it to my intended turnaround. Not a wise move. Five agonizing minutes later, I started eyeing trees to crouch behind. It was late evening and already quite dark, with not many passing cars to bear witness. It had distinct possibilities. Instead, I ultimately decided that leaves couldn't amply serve as toilet paper, so bravely, if not also miserably, I trudged forward. A half mile farther and I was considering knocking on a random front door in a neighborhood along Terrell Mill Road, hoping that the occupants would take pity on me and allow the quick use of their facilities. But it was right at dinnertime, and I'm nothing if not too polite to interrupt a family's meal.

Onward I plodded, now thankful that I was at least wearing black shorts. And just when I was debating how ugly this could get, the most beautiful sight came into view: I don't think that I have ever been so thrilled to see the golden arches of McDonald's. In a continuation of what had long ago been amended to a tempo run, I sprinted past the cashiers and patrons, all sporting puzzled stares, and made it into the stall with little, if any, time to spare. Had there been a line, the story wouldn't have ended quite so happily. As it was, following the pit stop that allowed my digestive tract to regain some semblance of normalcy, I completed the remaining two miles with little incident.

Experiences like these have taught me to just keep running while adopting a March-madness mentality of survive and advance, a sense of badassness gaining hold with each misfortune overcome. The miles are thus transformed from mere numbers tallied in a log to the tales from which legends, however masochistic, are born—perhaps otherwise aptly known as Marathon Maniacs.

An Incredible and Life-Changing Journey

by • Ed Loy

The journey of 26.2 miles has been an incredible and life-changing one for me. I started out the first 25 years of my life as a couch potato and was severely depressed, almost to the point of suicide. My journey began when I told someone about my resolution to lose weight. I was in my final semester in college, and I had just celebrated my 24th birthday. After many months of working to shed 25 pounds through walking, I decided to take up jogging to drop the weight faster. It was very challenging at first, but I kept at it and eventually crossed the barrier for the 10K. I saw myself as a runner and continued to plug away at my recent successes. I didn't love running right away, but I did love the feeling of getting outside and the feeling after a run.

After reading more about running and long-distance racing, I discovered the half-marathon. I thought I could do this to see where my fitness level was. My first half-marathon was on Maui in September 2007.

I loved the whole race atmosphere and the start. The course was tough and challenging for me, but I clocked in at a respectable 3:01:17 for my first time out. It was purely amazing! With a love for racing, I signed up for my first marathon, which was three months later. I thought to myself, *I can do this.*

When the race came, it was much harder than I had expected. I did not prepare for it the way marathoners usually prepare, with long runs and carboloading. Along the course, I had to sit down and take long rests. I managed to finish my first marathon in 8:49:48.

Since that fateful day, running has been an essential part of my lifestyle. I tried to forget the experience of my first marathon by getting better and preparing better. I qualified for the Marathon Maniacs by doing three marathons in 90 days.

Since receiving my signature yellow singlet, I have traveled much more than before. Seeing new cities I wouldn't have seen if it weren't for the marathon is just plain indescribable. Meeting fellow Marathon Maniacs is priceless, too. I remember running the San Francisco Marathon in 2009 wearing my yellow singlet. Many people screamed "Maniac!" at me. For a few seconds, I looked behind me and thought, *Who are they yelling at?* But now, I realized, they were yelling at me!

Being a marathoner has helped shape my entire well-being. The marathon has given me the tools to be a better person and has given me the desire to succeed in any endeavor I attempt.

I can now say with confidence that I love to run.

Postscript: *In 2011, Ed will be doing 13 states and his first double (back-to-back days). He hopes to reach 50 marathons by December 2012 at the Honolulu Marathon, where he will request a special bib number to commemorate the occasion.*

Marathon Maniac Quest

by • **Kim Heimbecker** • **Rick Deaver and** • **Elizabeth Culver**

We were training for our third marathon, the San Antonio Rock 'n' Roll. While on a long training run, we began discussing the marathons that we were thinking of doing that season. Elizabeth (Lyz) had signed up for four marathons to run with other friends, but one had developed a stress fracture and the other had work commitments, so unfortunately neither could go. After finding out that Lyz would be running the marathons alone, Kim and Rick signed up the next day to run the same four marathons, not knowing how we would train to get there. That started our quest to become Marathon Maniacs. We managed to complete the San Antonio Rock 'n' Roll on a very warm, humid November day.

The Dallas White Rock Marathon was next on our list and would be here in four short weeks. We were unsure of how to train for marathons so close together but were going to wing it. Fortunately, the weather was much cooler in December, and we had a great experience in Dallas. Still with no injuries, we continued to wing our way to the next marathon: Houston in January.

In Houston, Kim and Rick became separated from Lyz in the crowd around mile six and did not see her until the finish. Later, from our times on the course, we learned that she had passed us and was ahead of us until somewhere around mile 18, where we passed her without knowing it! We all finished with personal-best times and became Marathon Maniacs at the same time.

Now we had one more to go: Austin in February. Although it was a very hilly course, we completed it, while at the same time completing the Marathons of Texas Challenge.

But we were not done! Rick felt that he could do two more, and after much arm-twisting (not!), the three Maniacs signed up for two more marathons. However, plans do not always work out as anticipated. Kim had vacation plans that did not allow her to run Seabrook with Lyz and Rick, so she signed up for Cowtown and ran it 13 days after Austin. After running Seabrook, we had each run five marathons with one more to go. We ran Big D in our Marathon Maniac shirts and had a blast knowing that we were about to complete six marathons in six months and be silver-level Maniacs.

Although we enjoy running and training for marathons, we love running them together most of all. The exhilaration of finishing a marathon is made even better when shared with friends! Our journey continues.

The Benefits of Running in a Small Place

by • Gary Allen

Most of my life's running has been done on Great Cranberry Island, Maine. It is a small offshore island accessible only by boat. The main road is a very short two miles long. I have logged over 75,000 miles on this tiny island. My family settled here back in the late 1600s. I am 12th generation.

I firmly believe that running in such a small place has helped me become a much better runner than if I had had miles of open road in which to train. As we all know, a good part of running is in your head, and although I didn't know it at the time, as I ran back and forth during all those years, I was developing extraordinary mental toughness. I was recently honored to be included in a very short list of runners who have run sub-three-hour marathons in five consecutive decades (*http://www.arrs.net/TR_5Decades.htm*).

Two of those listed are Olympians Barry Magee and Vladimir Kotov, who ran for New Zealand and the Soviet Union respectively in 1960 and 1980. Magee was the bronze-medal winner behind barefoot Abebe Bikila in the Rome Olympic Marathon, and Kotov won the Soviet Olympic Trials and finished fourth in the Moscow Games. To say that I'm humbled would be an understatement, but I also couldn't help but notice that I am the only runner listed whose fifth decade is faster than his first.

I attribute my longevity and modest success to my roots but also to my training in such a confined space. I have always observed what others do, and I noticed that many runners' careers were quite short. I knew for certain that I didn't want to be like them and have basically done the opposite of what I saw many of them doing.

I decided at some point in my running career to become an experiment of one and to write my own rules for training. I firmly believe that my tried-and-true training techniques would no doubt help many run better and run longer, much as Yasso 800s help many runners go faster. I look forward to sharing my tips, philosophies, and practices with others. Until then, best of luck with the book!

Postscript: *Gary logged another sub-three-hour time at Boston in 2011, which moved him up to 14th on the all-time-span list (his first sub-three-hour marathon was completed in July 1978).*

Maniac Questionnaire

by • (The Reverend) Don Kienz

State you live in: Borderline nuts—oh, Pennsylvania.

How many marathons/ultramarathons have you run? 26/0 (that 0 is no accident), but once, after a marathon, I had to run a lot in the airport, so I was kind of wondering if we could have a third category. How many marathons have I run? Not a blessed one. It has been "Go out a bit too fast, run to exhaustion, and then shuffle-jog-walk just as fast as I can and possibly limp those last nine miles."

What was the first race you ever ran (any distance)? Age 10, eight kids, a quarter mile around the block, organized the event myself. Had a brand-new stopwatch.

What was the first marathon you ever ran? What year did you run it? Did you have fun that day? January 2003, age 47, Disney. Mickey wrapped the medal around my neck himself. I still get chills thinking about it. Afterward, walked like the Tin Man for four days. Curbs were impossible. Of course, I loved it. All 5:42 of it. Ran through Cinderella's Castle, high-fived Goofy and Donald Duck, even kissed Mary Poppins.

How long have you been a runner, and why did you start running? True story. August 2001, to encourage my sons to get fit like 46-year-old Dad, I jogged on the beach for four minutes straight. The next day, 4 minutes and 30 seconds. But it was New Year's Eve when my golfing friend announced that we would run a marathon in 2002. I just laughed. But on January 1, 2002, I made the one New Year's resolution of my life that I ever truly kept.

Why did you decide to become a Maniac? Or what inspired you? I hit the lotteries of both the Marine Corps and the New York City Marathons in my first year of marathoning. They are held one week apart, so I decided to run the MCM and postpone the following week's NYC to the next year.

Some vendor at the Marine Corps Marathon expo said to me, "Nah, you can run tomorrow and New York next weekend." Fifteen minutes later, another vendor said the same thing. Conclusion: vendors don't read running books.

So I ran and finished Marine Corps (fairly teary-eyed approaching the Iwo Jima Memorial), but with no leg muscles still functioning properly. The following Friday, I jogged five miles and came home with a grin on my face. My wife just laughed.

Saturday morning at the New York expo, I found four people wearing Marine Corps Marathon T-shirts, also giggling with total uncertainty, convincing each other that six hours would be *really* good.

At marker 24, one knee died. I hobbled to a 22-minute split for mile 25. Exhaustion, frustration, and disappointment turned into one last bit of determination. I created a stiff-legged, swing-it-out-and-around limp-jog for a 13-minute mile 26, to the rolling cheers of hundreds still lining 57th Street.

I had never felt more courageous in an athletic setting before.

After the finish, with a Mylar blanket and a medal around my neck, I stutter-stepped crosstown, and at least six random New Yorkers went out of their way to do the unheard of in New York: greet a stranger, congratulating me on completing the marathon. My 5:28? No one cared.

And thus, Maniac #48 was born.

Of all the races out there in this world, which one would you most like to run? Boston. Then London, Honolulu, anything in Switzerland, and the Great Wall when Mr. Yee goes back.

If you could run a marathon or ultra accompanied by anyone either living or deceased, whom would you choose and why? Two ideas. I am in enormous awe of the feats of the people in this club. Many have been inspiring: Olga, AnNie, Craig Holcomb, Chris, Tony, Steve, and on and on. So I keep my eye out for yellow singlets.

Unfortunately, after 200, 300 yards, I'm usually seeing singlets disappearing in the distance. So in a dream, I would choose Jesus of Nazareth. Then I would just listen.

What was your most memorable marathon and why?

1. Disney. It's just fun (and there was that Mary Poppins moment).

2. Marine Corps Marathon, every time. Stand up and take your hat off for a minute. It starts and ends in Arlington National Cemetery, passes every presidential memorial and the Capitol building, and finishes at the huge and sobering Iwo Jima Memorial. We live in freedom, and what did I ever do to secure that? So I spend four-plus hours feeling deeply grateful. It's a good feeling. It lasts, too.

3. New York. When you get to Manhattan at 16 and then again to Central Park at 23, there are a million screamin' people. It's New York, it feels like the World Series, and you are on the field: pretty cool.

If someone asked you to pick a race for a PR, which race would you suggest? Oh, Miami for certain. Can't understand why everybody doesn't do it. See, they have this choice thing set up. You can run a 26.2-mile marathon, or you can run a 13.1-mile marathon! Whew, cool! I really liked that; shoot, I think I'll be running one of those sub-three-hour marathons next year down there. This has really improved my chances for Boston!

What was the farthest you've ever traveled for a race? It was 3,000 miles from Philly to San Francisco, but I flew. I would nominate the 14-hour, 800-mile overnight drive from work in Philadelphia directly to Macon, Georgia, to run a 7:00 A.M. marathon on one hour of roadside sleep.

Do any of your nonrunning friends or family members think that you're crazy for running as much as you do? What are some of their comments to you? Crazy they knew well before running. Running for them is just a symptom.

If personal obligations or finances were not an issue, how many marathons would you run in one year? Zero. I would go play golf again, at *really* expensive golf courses. You ever been to TPC at Sawgrass? The 15th tee alone is paradise.

Well, maybe six or eight. (Or nine if Steve's going to China. If I've got the money, I'll even treat you to the plane ticket, Yee.)

From what race did you receive your favorite finisher's medal? True story. Context: I've entered 28 marathons, finished 26.

At the Self-Transcendence Marathon in August (I'm not a member of the spiritual mystics club that runs it, but they were the calmest people), I ran 12 miles and knew more miles that day would be dumb. Crossed 13.1, walked in, explained my adventure to this really nice medal lady, and asked her shyly if I could have a medal as a memento. She smiled one of those peaceful, happy smiles, congratulated me for finishing 13.1, and handed me a medal.

Restores your sense of hope, doesn't it?

Where do you keep your finisher's medals? The chiropractor insists that I need to remove them from my neck, but I've refused.

If you could put on a marathon anywhere in the world, where would you have it? The Monterey Peninsula. We would run the golf courses:

Poppy Hills, Pebble Beach, and the ultraprivate Cypress Point. We would be arrested, but we would run it.

Which race would you never run again and why? Oh, my. True story. I didn't do it, but it is the right answer.

There was this oceanworthy ship that sailed all the way to Antarctica with marathoners aboard, only to find out that the weather for the Antarctica Marathon was prohibitive. (Imagine the surprise.) So they ran around the deck of the ship for 26.2 miles.

Now, I didn't actually do that one, but some folks did, and if I *had* been one of them, I certainly wouldn't do it again.

What are your short-term running goals? Four hours. Shorter goal: keep getting out there. Each run is a victory in itself.

What are your long-term running goals? Boston. No, really—38 minutes to go (3:35). 🐱

What a Hobby

by • Craig Newport

When the number of marathons I had completed approached 100, friends of mine who thought it was a good thing asked how I had accomplished this.

Since I have more to be humble about than most runners, I won't presume to offer any running advice. There is plenty of that information available elsewhere. Instead, I made a of list of some issues facing the runner with a goal of running 100 marathons.

1. Choose your spouse carefully. I understand that Dr. Phil says this is a good idea for nonmarathoners, too. It is essential for the repetitive marathoner. Conversations with your spouse should avoid revealing how much money you have spent over the years on marathon entry fees, travel, lodging, shoes, and similar expenses.

2. Obtain employment that will allow you to wear marathon T-shirts and 80 percent worn-out running shoes as part of your normal business attire. Consider using marathon medals as jewelry.

3. Show no concern about how much "character" you have when you embark on your multimarathon quest. By the time you have completed 50 or 60 marathons, you will have endured enough rain-soaked,

wind-blown, porta-potty moments and other assorted embarrassing character-building experiences to last a lifetime.

4. Don't worry about training methods. There is some expert somewhere who has written a book validating whatever routine you stumble upon.

5. If your goal is to impress your nonrunning friends, run Boston a couple of times. Running the Boston Marathon has the same "wow" factor as running 20 other marathons. I understand that the Olympic Trials and the Olympics themselves also impress nonrunners, but I also notice that they involve drug testing. I never worked them into my schedule.

6. Keep your goals modest. Fewer than 1 percent of marathoners actually win the races they enter. Often you will find the same publicity hounds hogging the award stand more than once. I improved two minutes between marathon #1 and marathon #100. I anticipate being competitive with the current world-class times in roughly 900 years.

7. Obtain a nylon travel bag with zipper pockets on both ends. This allows you to keep your marathon instructions, motel reservations, and other paperwork separate from your Vaseline, shaving cream, sunscreen, and partially used motel soap.

8. Come to terms with the idea that you will have to increase your shoe size every decade or so. The alternative to this would be to decide that black toenails are attractive.

9. Avoid any fascination with British royalty. In the early 20th century, it was the royal family that influenced the lengthening to the current marathon distance at the London Olympics. When you get to mile 25 a few times and realize you could have been done, you may have negative thoughts toward the queen.

10. Acquire some running friends. As with most forms of compulsive behavior, you will need a network of enablers. A running club is an excellent place to find these people. Chances are that you will probably find members who are even more deranged than you.

Have fun.

How Did a Nonrunner Become a Marathon Maniac?

by • Bob Dolphin

Team Dolphin Marathon Maniac #32 happened because my wife, Lenore, is an avid supporter of my marathoning. Until recent heart problems, she hadn't missed any of my races since we first met 19 years ago. Lenore was there to support me, be a volunteer, and give hugs to many runners as they crossed the finish line. Her total attendance is now well over 333 marathons, and it was an honor for Team Dolphin to be inducted into the Marathon Maniacs Hall of Fame at the Yakima River Canyon Marathon (YRCM) on April 4, 2009.

There are over 4,000 running Maniacs and one Maniac who has "run" only 10 marathons in nine years and in a different way—she is the day-of-race director of the YRCM. This is how a nonrunner became a member.

On the ferry in Washington State from Friday Harbor to Anacortes the day after the June 2003 inaugural San Juan Island Marathon, Steve Yee asked me how many marathons I had run so far in 2003. The year before, I had run 24 marathons, and Steve wanted to outdo this old guy in 2003. He was disappointed that we both had just run marathon #11 and that both would be at the inaugural North Olympic Discovery Marathon the next weekend at Port Angeles, Washington.

At the Coeur d' Alene Marathon in Idaho the week before, a fellow runner had called Steve and his friends "Marathon Maniacs" for running so many in such a short time. The name sounded good to them, and an idea was born that was soon to give birth to something special.

Lenore and I have volunteered at packet pickup for 17 years at the Seattle Marathon each November. In 2003, Steve Yee, Chris Warren, and Tony Phillippi picked up their packets from us and then left some business cards with us to distribute for the new club they had just formed.

In January, Lenore sent a special bulletin to the members of the 100 Marathon Club North America, which we direct, and to her 50 States Marathon Club master list, informing everyone of the Marathon Maniacs club. Questions from Tony the next time he saw Lenore included, "Who is Cathy Troisi from New York?" "Who is Tom Detore from Nebraska?" She helped get the first members who weren't locals, and we are responsible for getting Roger Biggs as the first United Kingdom marathoner to join.

When I sent in my application for Maniac membership, I suggested that the club form an auxiliary for people who support marathons, as Lenore does. She had volunteered for 24 hours at a time for six consecutive years at the Pacific Rim 24-Hour Run in Longview, Washington. She had worked in almost all jobs at races for many years, was co-director of the YRCM, *and* at that time had attended over 200 marathons herself.

The response from the main Maniacs was, "She has been to more marathons than all three of us combined! We want her to be a part of the club." With the records they racked up in the seven years since, that couldn't be said now. Lenore has accompanied me to races near and far and has volunteered at marathons at Little Rock, New Orleans, Memphis, and many other places. It's great to share #32 with her and to have her as the nonrunning half of Team Dolphin.

The Purpose of Running

by • Kelsey Swift

In March 2009, I received a message from my best friend from high school. She was coming to town to run the Seattle Marathon in November and thought that I might like to sit with her parents and cheer her on.

Cheer? With her *parents*? No freakin' way!

I decided one week after my 36th birthday (March 14) that I would run that stinking race. This would shock the hell out of her because I had always made fun of her for "running without a purpose."

Having absolutely no running experience, I started out by setting very small goals. My first time out, I just wanted to jog once around the track. I was able to go five times without walking! I was psyched! It was on. I started asking for running advice and reading running books. I talked to a friend of a friend on Facebook (Nic Plemel), learned of a free marathon (Michelle's Grande Ass), and decided to run it for practice.

That is what really got me. Everyone out there was *so* nice and supportive! It was an incredible experience, and I wanted to do it again! I ran another marathon two weeks later so that I could join the Maniacs. The Marathon Maniacs community (and the feeling of accomplishment) made me understand the purpose of running. 🐈

Passing on to the Next World

by • Joe "Moonie" Arcilla

For me, running was initially for fitness. By my late 30s, I had reached a point where obesity was threatening to adversely affect my well-being if I didn't act.

I never suspected that running would become not only a passion but also something that I considered fun. That's a good foundation to become a Marathon Maniac, though my first marathon experience (a typical beginner's "too much, too soon" tale) suggested otherwise.

But the most satisfying thing to me about running is how life affirming it can be, with the sense of community shared among its participants. Never is that more evident than when a group member unexpectedly passes on to the next world.

Joe Truini ("Voodoo" or "Voo" to his friends) was a Maniac (#1522), but he was a member of many circles, running and otherwise, so when he passed away suddenly, in late July 2009, it shook many people.

Joe proved the notion about deceptive appearances. His flowing dreadlocks and muscular build didn't fit the runner's archetype. First glances had an element of intimidation (he even boxed in his younger days), but he was one of the easiest-going, kindest, and most intelligent people around.

He was paradoxically bigger than life and down to earth at the same time. Mere minutes of talking and sharing a beer with him after a race made you feel that you had known him your entire life.

Over the rest of the year, many fond memories and tributes were shared by those who knew him, including a get-together at the Outer Banks Marathon in November, the last race for which Joe had registered. I was in that close-knit circle of friends who gathered. We each had prepared both group and individual tributes. Fond memories and camaraderie were in plentiful supply. Those who couldn't make it sent their own gestures, from origami cranes to beer-kitty money.

In a sense, my tribute to Joe began when I signed up for OBX shortly after his passing. What was maniacal about that was the fact that I hadn't run longer than a half-marathon distance since 2007. Oh, and I had an appendectomy two months before and had barely returned to running.

As time went on, the scale of my tribute grew—I secretly signed up for and ran in a marathon two weeks prior . . . in a caveman costume (Joe regularly ran his hometown marathon in one).

Race day at Outer Banks was not promising; due to illness, I had managed only 10 miles of running in the two weeks between marathons. I ran with friends the whole way during the marathon, but unexpected warm temperatures and a bridge at mile 23

had us on the brink when we reached the mile-25 aid station.

This is where a sign—from above—gave us strength. We spotted a hand-drawn sign on a nearby garbage can asking, "What would Voo do?"

Joe, as tough a runner as anyone, would have had one answer for that: "Run!" And we did, all the way to the finish line.

And with that, I personally had reached Maniac status.

Thank you, Voo. Miss you, big guy!

Photos courtesy of Bob Mann

The Importance of Running

by • Ken Briggs

I'm taking the bait. I don't necessarily like talking about my running in this way, but perhaps my story will help someone else get or stay motivated.

I ran track in high school and college back in the 1960s and early '70s. I was a solid 880 runner (for you youngsters, that is just a bit over 800 meters!) and a fair miler. I quit running completely in 1971 to focus on school, partying, playing in bands, working, and smoking cigarettes (and other stuff). By 1991, I had finally tamed the vices but did not exercise in any regular fashion.

Fast forward to 2001. My 6-foot-2-inch frame was now carrying 225 pounds (track weight was 185); essentially, every physical measurement that was supposed to be up was down, and vice versa.

I picked up a copy of Andrew Weil's *Eight Weeks to Optimum Health*. One of his prescriptions was five 50-minute walks per week. I dove into it and started eating really well and walking everywhere. It was on one of these walks that I wondered whether I could run a little: I tried, but I couldn't go more than about 50 yards (or meters!). Yikes, here I was, 30 years since I had last run, 50 years old, and just pathetic. What to do?

Simple. Engage in male-pattern behavior and enter the Bloomsday 12K the next spring. What the heck, I had six months to get ready. I got myself some really good Spalding "running" shoes at the local discount place (they weighed about 2 pounds each!) and started training. Never mind that I had never run on the roads or had any idea what I was doing.

Well, after bouts with all the classic overuse injuries, I got myself into Runners Soul (our Spokane specialty-running store) and got fitted for my first real running shoes. Back in the day, running shoes were our track spikes. I thought distance runners were weird. I got a good training plan online and started my workouts. Well, I made it through that 2002 Bloomsday and then started running a few 5Ks and fun runs. Though I didn't have the leg turnover of a 20-year-old, I was competitive in my age group. I even entered some track events: humbling, but still competitive in the age group. Then I decided that a half-marathon might be a good goal. In spring 2003, I did the Coeur d'Alene Half-Marathon. (Little did I know that a group called Marathon Maniacs was born right then and there.)

Now I had the distance bug and entered the Spokane Marathon that October. Of course, upon finishing, I swore that I would never do that again! By now, I was reading everything I could and getting serious about my second running career. I had joined the local running club and started participating in races just about every weekend. The club members were really encouraging, and one member in particular, Jim Hoppe, really made me feel welcome on group runs. Jim and I have gone on to become good pals. I even won our yearlong series in 2004. Woo hoo—medals and plaques and trophies were coming in! And my weight was now down to a healthy 165!

I started running more marathons (and even some ultras), and in 2006 my friend Michael Wakabayashi (MM #20) was asking about my recent runs. I told him that I had run the Mount Hood 50-miler, the Uncle Joe 50K, and the Spokane Marathon. Mike said I was a Maniac; I said, "Same to you!" Then he explained that I had qualified as an MM. I joined that fall, and now I've run 62 marathons or longer. Last year I missed three while recovering from surgery to repair an inguinal hernia.

And this June, three days following a solid 100K, I found myself in the hospital having a 2-pound stromal tumor removed from behind my stomach. Six days in the hospital and seven transfusions left me pretty trashed. My prognosis is very good, though. The grade of my tumor makes it low risk for spread or recurrence: no chemo or radiation, just blood tests every three months and a CT scan in six months as a precaution.

I am very fortunate, and four weeks after surgery, I am running (a little) again. Running has become very important to my physical and mental well-being, and being a Marathon Maniac has given me a way to focus on running. Having that singlet on at races helps open many conversations. The friends I've met in the club and the stories I've heard have been very inspirational.

There are some real heroes in our group. And, yes, I'm planning to run the Grand Ridge 50K on August 7, if I'm strong enough.

The Greatest Reward

by • Kristine M. Jahn

Twelve years ago I never dreamed that I would be an athlete, much less a marathoner. I was always the fat kid, the very fattest of fat kids, the 300-pound kid.

Most kids grew up with soccer, baseball, and Scouts. I grew up with Entenmann's and Hostess. In junior high and high school, the kids called me "Manhattan" because—as they put it—I was as big as the island. From about age 14 on, every visit to my doctor, whether for a routine exam or the flu, was marked with a notation of "morbid obesity." By age 22, I weighed 380 pounds—my highest recorded weight.

In May 1998, just after completing my first year of law school, I took a trip out East with my best friend. After a week of nonstop eating and drinking, it was there, in a Friendly's restaurant, that something

snapped. While spooning a peanut butter cup sundae into my mouth, I told my friend that I would lose the weight once I returned home from the trip. It was as simple as that in my mind.

And I did lose weight. I began a yearlong liquid-protein diet in June 1998, just before my 23rd birthday. The goal was not simply to lose weight but to change my life. I was determined to do it on my own without any type of invasive surgery. And to prove that I was truly committed, I started a six-day-per-week exercise regimen right from the start. I was amazed at how much energy I developed as my exercise increased.

A year later, I had lost 225 pounds and had gained a wealth of knowledge on nutrition, exercise, and healthy living—all of the tools that I would need to ensure that my lifestyle change was a permanent one.

With the weight off, it was time to find a new challenge to ensure that I stayed motivated to keep it off.

I didn't become a runner immediately. I had never run more than a few steps in my entire life. including while I was losing weight. But I remembered a day in ninth grade when Kevin Hanson (of the Hansons-Brooks Distance Project) came into my gym class and told us that we were all going to try to run three-quarters of a mile the next day. He was recruiting for the high school girls' cross-country team. I was determined—at nearly 300 pounds—to finish the run.

The next morning, I crossed the starting line and made it about 30 yards before giving up. I remembered that moment sometime in mid-1999, and I decided that I would give running a shot. My first race was in late 1999. I ran the 2.2-mile aptly named Ambulance Chase at my law school. It took me about 27 minutes, but I ran every step of it! All of my law school classmates were there to cheer me on. For the next year, I stayed around three miles per run, a few times a week, running alone before my gym opened in the morning.

In fall 2000, I met the Rick's Runners gang—a local group of friendly runners that ran as early as I did and were members of my gym. On the day I met them, they conned me into running three miles alongside them, despite my protest that I was way too slow to run with other people. I was immediately hooked! And in spite of never having run more than 3.5 miles up until that point, I ran my first 10K only 10 days later.

It wasn't long before I had the marathon bug and completed my first marathon—the 2001 Chicago Marathon. And my second—the 2002 Chicago Marathon. After finishing my first marathon, I decided that I would run at least 50 marathons before my 50th birthday—and maybe an ultramarathon or even an Ironman. It happened quickly; I had become a marathon junkie. To date I've completed 26 marathons, including my first Saturday/Sunday double in December 2009. Since I met up with the Marathon Maniacs in 2009, my marathon addiction has kicked in full force. Even with a career, a husband, and two young kids, I managed at least one marathon a month in 2010.

Most of my marathon times are not very speedy. They are something a little different, something very personal to me. I have accomplished many goals with much support and encouragement. It's my turn to give back. During most of my marathons, I find a few first-timers or people who appear to be struggling, and I run with them, maybe for a few miles, sometimes an entire race. I help them pass the time and encourage them to keep going.

In the end, we finish. And that's my reward—knowing that I was there to help someone else finish.

And I will keep doing that because that's the greatest reward—motivating and encouraging others to accomplish their goals. This is what keeps me motivated and helps me conjure up new goals, such as completing a 100-mile ultramarathon and an Ironman by my 40th birthday.

Congratulations, Maniacs!

by • Barefoot Jon

The trials and tribulations of training, injuries, and so on, to say nothing of personal/business/family-time management, are a cause to celebrate when you complete the necessary three-in-three-months or two-in-two-weeks entry-level marathons to become a Marathon Maniac. For some Maniacs, however, it wasn't that extraordinary, just something to do when time permitted in their busy lives.

Marathon Maniac #985—Francesca the Italian—was in awe of men and women running a 100K through her hometown mountains before she settled in the United States to raise her family with her Irish husband. As time permitted, she entered local 5K and 10K fun runs every year along with a half-marathon a couple of blocks from her home in Woodinville, Washington.

Then, at the 5K Resolution Run in 2008, she decided that it was time to run a 100K race, which is what had gotten her started running in the first place. Francesca had already done a marathon a couple of years earlier without any adverse effects. As far she was concerned, she was ready. But most of her friends figured that she needed a dose of reality for the substantial training that is usually required for a 100K race, so she agreed to enter a 50-miler.

The 50-miler didn't faze her, and in the following month, she chalked up another 50 miles in a 12-hour run and then breezed to her first 100K two weeks later. Without even knowing it, she became one of the few Marathon Maniacs who qualified only on the basis of ultramarathons. Congratulations!

Marathon Maniac #1105, Butterfly Princess Mariposai, is originally from Paraguay, where her love of the outdoors was stifled due to the traditional household responsibilities required of women. In a Portland bookstore 20 years ago with her husband, she watched star struck for more than 20 minutes as thousands of thin-clad men and women streamed by along the street in front of them.

"What are they doing?" she asked her husband. "Oh, it's just a marathon," he replied. It turned out to be much more than just a marathon for him, too, when he watched her finish the Portland Marathon in 2006. In fact, he was so proud of his wife's accomplishment that when work and home commitments prevented adequate training for the following year's marathon, he signed her up for another nearby marathon as a surprise training-run gift. Inadvertently, this led to her Marathon Maniac qualification #1105. Congratulations, Butterfly Princess.

Marathon Maniac #685, Erika Van Flein, didn't realize that her yearly hometown Equinox Marathon was one of the hardest in the country, so she hardly noticed when an out-of-town trip two weeks earlier coincided with another town's marathon. However, her friends noticed, and she became the first Alaska Marathon Maniac. Congratulations, Erika!

Charity Running

by • Brian Joachims

I participated in my first endurance event about a week before my 40th birthday. It had nothing to do with my age but everything to do with meeting a challenge.

A friend of mine at work commented that she and a group of her friends were going to walk the half-marathon at the 2007 Oklahoma City Memorial Marathon. Having been a walker for fitness for several years, I had never even considered doing an actual event. I got online, looked at the details, and made up my mind that I could do it. A few months and a lot of training miles later, I walked every step of the 13.1 miles. I finished in 3 1/2 hours with a few blisters on my feet and sore muscles everywhere—and a tremendous sense of accomplishment.

I immediately thought, *Hey, I can do more of this.* I signed up for a 5K run within the next couple of weeks and walked and ran that event in a little over 36 minutes (I had yet to hear about Jeff Galloway or John Bingham or a walk-run training method). I continued to participate in more events, running some and walking some. For each event, there was a bag of goodies. Generally, these had some-percentage-off-merchandise promotions at the local running store, or sometimes a water bottle, but always the obligatory T-shirt.

But in one goody bag there was a flyer for The Leukemia & Lymphoma Society's Team in Training. One of the events it was training for was the Walt

Disney World Marathon. I have been a Disney lover since early childhood and thought that if I were going to try to stay on my feet for an incredible 26.2 miles, Disney World should be the place to do it. So I attended an information meeting and signed up not only to participate in a marathon but also to raise a few thousand dollars for charity along the way.

That was the beginning of what has become an incredible journey of endurance training, events, and fund-raising for victims of blood cancers. I have completed several more marathons since that time plus 100-mile bicycle rides, ultramarathons, half-marathons, duathlons, triathlons, and a half-iron-distance triathlon.

Other than the events themselves, I think that what I enjoy the most is when people call me "crazy," "nuts," or "insane" for continuing to do this. That is what made joining the Marathon Maniacs a natural fit for me.

Marathon

by • Claire Carder

Written on the plane from Omaha, Nebraska, to Portland, Oregon, after doing the Marathon to Marathon and Swan Lake double in June 2010.

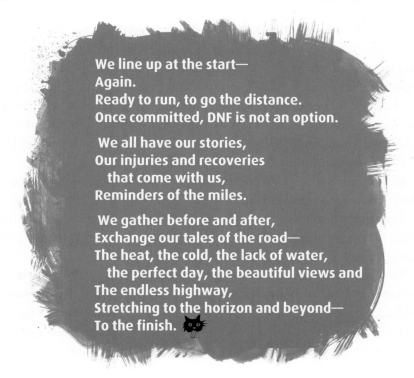

We line up at the start—
Again.
Ready to run, to go the distance.
Once committed, DNF is not an option.

We all have our stories,
Our injuries and recoveries
    that come with us,
Reminders of the miles.

We gather before and after,
Exchange our tales of the road—
The heat, the cold, the lack of water,
    the perfect day, the beautiful views and
The endless highway,
Stretching to the horizon and beyond—
To the finish.

Getting Married on the Run

by • David Stout

My wife, Vicki, and I met at a half-marathon in Kansas City in 2003. We fell in love and soon after moved together to Seattle. I hadn't run a marathon in a long time (nine years), but Vicki decided that since we lived in the great Northwest, we should start doing so. We ran Crater Lake and Seattle and a few others. As we began running, we saw the ubiquitous Maniac shirts and knew that we had to join. In 2006, we ran three marathons in three months and became Marathon Maniacs #290 and #291. I said at the time, and I still do, "If you live long enough, you'll find a club to belong to."

We got engaged in 2006 and planned a sizable wedding that was to include our kids and extended families. On a lark, we decided to run the Las Vegas Marathon together in December 2006. I saw a special deal on the website where you could stop at mile 5.5 and get married by the "runnin' reverend."

Well, since running is what we do and where we met, this seemed like a perfect match for us. Vicki balked, however. She insisted that "Someone would take a picture of us, or we would get in the newspaper, or worse, be on television getting married," and our families would find out. I assured her that we weren't going to be the center of attention, that some young couple with an appetite for publicity would catch the eye of the *paparazzi*, and that we would fade into the background.

So we sent in our bio and application, and lo and behold, we were accepted. The day of the marathon dawned, and all decked out in white and black with the garter on Vicki's leg, we teed it up in front of the Mandalay Bay. We ran the 5.5 miles with the Running Elvises and at the Special Memory Wedding Chapel, we stopped and tied the knot. As I had predicted, a couple from Savannah, Georgia, that had made the trek with an entourage was the center of all the media attention. We completed the marathon, and at the finish we were elated, fatigued, and ecstatic. The Running Elvises, who had also served as our witnesses, were at the finish to congratulate us and get in our wedding photos. What a wonderful day. We went back to Seattle still planning to have a traditional wedding with friends and family and to keep this event as our special secret.

About three months passed. In March, I began to get strange e-mails and messages from old friends and acquaintances. The gist was, "I didn't know you were getting married," or "I saw that you got married; why no announcement?" At work, our deputy counsel came through the office with a magazine in his hand saying, "Hey, our auditor is in *Runner's World*."

Uh, oh. I cringed. Sure enough, there it was in the March 2007 *Runner's World*, page 19. There is the picture of the couple from Georgia right in the middle of a two-page spread about 4 inches tall. To the right in the foreground, there we are, our picture about 8 inches tall, *getting married at the Las Vegas Marathon*. As my kids would say, "OMG." Needless to say, while I tried to keep the noise down, it was useless. My daughter called and said, "My friend said she saw you and Vicki in a magazine getting married." We were exposed. We ended up sending out copies of the magazine to everyone along with our explanation. After Vicki got over the shock and forgave me (I am the luckiest guy in the world), she came around to agreeing that having 700,000 wedding pictures in circulation is certainly unique and, actually, pretty cool.

This will always be my most unforgettable marathon, much bigger than Boston or New York or Big Sur. 🐱

Life of a Marathon Couple

by • Dave and Linda Major

Linda was born with a hole in her heart, and Dave has lived with asthma since he was 2 years old—not what you would call perfect human specimens built for marathon running!

Before meeting Dave, Linda had never run. Her first marathon in 2001 was supposed to be a one-off. She soon realized, after entering a marathon in 2003, that completing 20-mile training runs was harder than running a marathon every couple of weeks. In 2006, she ran her 100th marathon in Munich, Germany, dancing the conga across the finish line with 20 other 100 Marathon Club friends.

Linda has won numerous prizes in her age category, but one of her most memorable achievements was placing first veteran woman (age 35 to 45) in the marathon of Bilbao. It was memorable because she was going to pull out at halfway due to the heat and humidity; numerous other runners were walking back to the start, numbers ripped off and despondent. The old adage of the tortoise and the hare could never have been more accurate than on this occasion.

Linda has set targets for herself every year, combining charity fund-raising with pushing her own limitations. Apart from raising approximately $15,000, she has moved from running just marathons to running triple marathons and ultras that take one whole day to complete.

Her proudest achievement was completing the 2008 Comrades ultra-marathon in South Africa. In 2009, Linda was crowned the third Marathon Maniacs Lady with a total of 52 marathons and became the first woman in the UK to be awarded 10 stars (Titanium level) and only the second person from the UK to receive this award, after her husband, Dave. She has now run in more than 32 countries and recently completed her 300th marathon, becoming only the second woman in the UK to reach this milestone.

In 1994, Dave was an overweight smoker with compounding health problems. He was told that he had only five years left to live if didn't change his ways dramatically. Initially, stopping smoking and beginning a diet was the easier part of the deal. *What am I going to do socially for the rest of my life?* was the hardest thing for Dave to think through.

Dave started running on September 1, 1994. He ran 100 yards down the street before he turned back. In Ireland, 10 years later almost to the day, he ran his 100th marathon. In 2004, when Linda started to run marathons regularly, Dave started to complete marathons almost weekly.

Since 2006, Dave has averaged a marathon every week. He has participated in numerous ultramarathons, with his most memorable achievement, like Linda's, being Comrades in 2008. Dave's and Linda's race experiences are pretty similar with regard to the countries they have visited, their favorite races, and the toughest ones they have attempted, although Dave has never picked up an award in any of his age groups. The nearest he came was

finishing fourth in the Cayman Islands; he had been in third place, but he stopped for a beer at 25 miles. "I was not disappointed with the time it took me to savor the ice-cold beer in the 85-degree-Fahrenheit heat; it made up for me missing the podium." This comment perfectly sums up how Dave views his marathon aims and goals.

Dave's proudest achievements have been placing as the third Maniac in 2008 and the second Maniac in 2009, with 52 and 59 marathons, respectively. Running one marathon a week didn't even get you a top-three place in the 2009 Marathon Maniacs listing, and with more marathons and Maniacs coming on the scene continually, Dave thinks that 60-plus marathons will be needed in future years to get in the top three.

Running in Europe regularly, they have been fortunate to make acquaintances in many different countries. Their style of marathon running is a welcoming, all-inclusive experience with everyone competing for their own, sometimes personal reasons. At the same time, a common thread connects all marathon runners, irrespective of any language or cultural barriers.

Linda and Dave want to continue their marathon journey with health, fitness, and happiness as their main focus. They have recently applied for the world record for the most marathons completed by a married couple, although like all records, it's just a statistic.

They both got off to an unlucky start with their health, but they're going to make the most of what they have rather than complain about what they were not given.

As actions speak louder than words, Dave and Linda recently launched *www.madeyarun.com*, a running-travel company. It's a subscription service that hosts not-for-profit tours on a regular basis. Dave and Linda began their business because they were alarmed at the prices some tour companies were charging to travel to events that were open to everyone. They use their 750-plus marathons and knowledge of visiting places to help clients achieve their goals.

Dave sometimes gets annoyed when people say they can't run. Very few people are unlucky enough to be physically incapable of running. Running gave him back his life and has prolonged it, too. If through their actions they improve the lives of those genuinely unable to participate, then that is a worthy cause in its own right.

Crossing the Finish Line

by • Kim Williamson

On November 26, 2008, at 12:33 P.M., I received a phone call that changed my life. I heard four dreadful words: "You have breast cancer." I live in Portland, Oregon, but I was across the country in Atlanta, Georgia, for the Thanksgiving Day marathon that I was supposed to run the very next day. After I processed the startling news, the reality was hitting me that I had cancer and that I might not be able to run for a while. I had run four marathons that year and Atlanta was to be my fifth, my eighth lifetime marathon. I had qualified for the Marathon Maniacs club earlier that year when I ran the Goofy Challenge in Orlando, and two weeks later I ran the Miami Marathon. Finding out that I had cancer at 37 years of age stunned me. I was healthy, I exercised, I ate healthily, I lifted weights, and I had no family history of cancer—this can't be happening to me. The thought of not running more marathons disturbed me. How can cancer take that from me? So even though I did not sleep at all that night, I decided that I would run the marathon despite my diagnosis because I was afraid that it would be my last marathon.

Nineteen hours after that fateful phone call, I was at the starting line of the Atlanta Thanksgiving Day marathon. I ran it with my boyfriend, William (MM #1871); it was an emotionally tough race. I would run and cry, run and cry, but William kept me going. I hit a wall and just about gave up around mile 20, but somehow I found a burst of determination in the last two miles and sprinted to the finish line. We finished 1 1/2 minutes under the five-hour cutoff and exactly 24 hours after my diagnosis. After we crossed the finish line, William took the medal from the volunteer before she could put on me. He placed it around my neck and said, "Now you start the race for your life."

I did race for my life. Three weeks after the Atlanta Marathon, I had the first of five operations to remove the cancer and reconstruct the breasts. I endured four months of chemotherapy, six weeks (28 rounds) of radiation, and a couple of trips to the emergency room. Needless to say, 2009 was a tough year. But in January 2010, I ran the Miami Marathon, logging my ninth marathon and first postcancer race. Three weeks later, I ran the Breast Cancer Marathon in Jacksonville, Florida. In March 2010, I had two final operations, and six weeks later I joined my fellow Maniacs at the Tacoma Marathon Maniac reunion on May 2, 2010.

Running a marathon tests our endurance, plays games with our minds, and pushes our bodies beyond what we thought possible. It turns out that cancer treatment follows a similar pattern. And now, crossing the finish line has a whole new meaning to me.

I am a runner, I am a Marathon Maniac, and I am a cancer survivor. 🐱

24

Marathon Maniac Friendship

by • Marie Zornes

I first heard about the Marathon Maniacs when I ran into Patch Dahl's wife at the mall. Patch and I had just run our first marathon a couple of months before, and she told me that Patch had run three more since then. *What*?

He wanted to join this club called the Marathon Maniacs. I thought it was crazy, but I looked into it anyway. That's when I learned that it *was* crazy—done with that!

Well, it took me a couple of years, but I decided that I would give it a try. Boy, am I glad that I did. I have made more friends than I can think of. If I were not a Marathon Maniac, I would have met these people, and that would have been the end of it; I probably would not have met them again. But that is not the case when you are a Marathon Maniac.

The first friends that I think of are Jane Herzog and Ray Shaw. Jane was my best friend when I was in second grade, but I had not seen her since high school graduation. We reconnected at the Tacoma City Marathon. I was not a Maniac yet, but Jane was, and Ray was qualifying that day. I have traveled with them to several races and participated in many more that they are at. It is always great to see them.

When I became a Maniac, I thought that I would never wear the singlet. I ran a lot of the Seattle Marathon with Paul Gentry. He was qualifying that day. He showed me the beauty of wearing Maniac gear. He shouted out to every Maniac we encountered along the Interstate 90 bridge. I saw the camaraderie that goes along with being a Maniac. How could I have been so foolish before? To this day, I love out-and-backs just for that reason, seeing the Maniac friends that I already have and those that I have yet to meet.

Also, being a Maniac makes me think of my friend Tory Klemensten. We met at Coeur d'Alene. We were running about the same pace. We chatted and ended up running almost the entire race together. We have since met at and run too many races to count. She is an inspiration to many, and I am lucky to count her as my friend.

Who would have thought that you could become such good friends with people you meet on the bus ride to the start of the race? I have a couple. The first one is Dana Peters. We sat together on the bus to the start of the Maui Marathon. We never saw each other during the race but met up again at the finish. On the bus ride, I mentioned that I wanted to do Goofy. She said that she would if I did. We met back at Maui the next year and then at Goofy. We have also met up at several other marathons.

Also on the bus, this time at Light at the End of the Tunnel, I met Betsy Rogers and Matt Hagen. We did not meet up again for about a year, but we have since become great friends. I have also traveled with both of them many times, and there is never a shortage of laughter. They are a great couple to hang out with and run with.

There are many more friends; the list just goes on and on.

If you are not a Maniac yet, I strongly encourage you to join this club. It is the greatest! 🐱

True Confessions of a Marathon Maniac

by • Marsha White

I didn't start out to be a Marathon Maniac. Heck, I never even thought about doing a race, let alone a marathon, until I went through a personal crisis several years ago. I lost my appetite and so, instead of eating lunch during my break at work, I went for a walk. I walked faster and faster to work out the demons plaguing me. A coworker who also happened to be a runner saw me during one of these sessions and suggested that I enter one of the races sponsored by the Florida Track Club here in Gainesville. I laughed and retorted that those races were for runners and that I was simply a walker who was kind of fast.

But the seed was planted.

I entered my first race that fall, a half-marathon in the small neighboring town of Micanopy. Walking the entire way, I finished in less than three hours—how exhilarating! My husband met me at the finish line and listened to me gloat about how wonderful I felt and how I could hardly wait to do another race. His response was, "Now, don't get carried away!" Fortunately, I didn't listen to him. I completed my first full marathon in January 2007 at Disney World, and since that time I have completed 61 marathons and ultras in 45 states. My longest streak has been six marathons in six weeks, including a six-hour timed race.

In 2007, I finished six marathons and by early 2008 had 10 under my belt, including three in less than three weeks. This meant that I could now join the Maniacs as well as the 50 States Marathon Club and the 50 States & DC club. I promptly sent in my statistics and membership fee for all three groups.

Timed races are my favorites—I like finishing with everyone else at the end of a race. Speed is not my thing, but I have the endurance to walk for a long time, so I am now intrigued by ultramarathons. I have already completed several 50K races and an eight-hour track race and will attempt my first 12-hour event this summer. I have also discovered trail racing. Falling is much easier on my body when it happens on dirt or pine needles instead of asphalt!

So now, at the age of 64, I am a confirmed athlete. Everyone in my family and most of the folks at work think I am completely crazy. I reassure them that I am *not* crazy; I am just a confirmed Marathon Maniac!

Hope, Strength, Determination, Courage

by • Megan Ross Hope

The idea came to me earlier that year. With five previous marathons completed, I was ready for the next level: to run two marathons on back-to-back weekends. I chose the fall lineup of the Bellingham Bay Marathon and the Portland Marathon and set an additional goal to raise money for the Children's Tumor Foundation (CTF), an organization that funds research for neurofibromatosis (NF), a genetic disease that I have. This story is about the Portland Marathon on October 4, 2009.

NF has caused dozens of tumors all over my body, and I have had three operations to remove tumors on the right side of my face and ear canal. Facing the disease gives me the strength to keep putting one foot in front of the other, mile after mile, and running marathons gives me the courage to face this progressive disease year after year.

Wearing my neon-yellow CTF jersey, I lined up at the starting line, my body still sore from the previous week's marathon. My only goal was to cross the finish line. Ahead of me stood a racer in a Marathon Maniac jersey—little did he know that I was soon to join his ranks with a back-to-back weekend finish.

Early in the race I held back, enjoying the spirited spectators and the company of fellow runners. The comfortable pace was easy to maintain, and at the half I was on target for a 4 hour, 45 minute finish, a typical race pace for me. But something inside of me turned on, and at that moment I sped up, left the pace group behind, and never looked back. The last six miles are tough for anyone running a marathon, and I knew that I was breaking down. I sailed through the downhill between miles 21 and 23, repeating this mantra: *hope, strength, determination, courage.*

By mile 25, I was physically exhausted. With my stomach churning, lungs near capacity, and a worn-out body, I dashed for the finish line: *hope, strength, determination, courage. Follow it all the way to the end.* And I did it. I crossed the line at 4:29:29—a PR by 14 minutes and a negative split for the second half. Much to my surprise, the second marathon in seven days turned out to be the best marathon of my life! In that moment, I was too tired to cry in celebration, so I received my finisher's medal, wobbled my way toward the food tables, and promptly stuffed my face with bananas, oranges, apples, cookies, water, and anything else lying around.

Neurofibromatosis pushes down on me, so I push back. I am determined to continue pushing, pursuing more marathons and eventually an ultra, while also fighting for access to health insurance and another operation.

While many of those I speak with cannot see themselves running a marathon, I see an opportunity to use this mantra: *hope, strength, determination, courage.* Let it take you places you never thought possible.

27

Running to Heal

by • Paul C. David

The summer of 2008 had been shaping up nicely. I was a newly minted Marathon Maniac, and I had my next several races picked out already. But things didn't go according to plan.

On July 1, I woke up early, kissed my wife good-bye, and got on my bike to ride to work. Six days later I woke up in the intensive care unit at Harborview Hospital in Seattle. I had been hit by a careless driver in a pickup truck. I had many broken bones and a collapsed lung and had lost the vision in one eye. Most seriously, I had suffered a traumatic brain injury, requiring surgery to save my life. I spent a month in the hospital and most of the month after that in bed.

Those early months were very hard. I required full-time care and couldn't walk more than a few minutes at a time. Even the most basic activities wiped me out. There are no guarantees and no schedules for recovery from a traumatic brain injury.

Along the way, I received an incredible degree of love and support from family and friends. My running friends spent many hours with me, in the hospital and at home. There is something extraordinary about relationships forged on the trails, mile by mile. With family and friends like mine, I had no excuse not to focus on getting strong. The gift of hope is powerful.

Things began to improve as fall began. I focused on what I could do—initially, to simply get up and around. Soon I was walking everywhere I could, from home to doctors' appointments to physical therapy, walking over 30 miles per week. Just after Thanksgiving, I walked the Seattle Half-Marathon, my first distance event since the accident. Then I knew that I would be able to cover the miles again.

I began running again in December. My first group run started on a bitter-cold and snowy morning. I worried about simply being able to keep up. But three weeks later, I ran the Nookachamps Half-Marathon, north of Seattle. It wasn't fast, but I felt very good about my effort.

On April 4, just over nine months after the accident, I lined up to do the Yakima River Canyon Marathon. My training ramp had been a bit steep, and I needed to walk a bit. But I crossed the finish in just over four hours, and I knew that I was just starting. By the time New Year's Day rolled around, I had completed 11 marathons and ultras. Along the way, I set a personal best and had run my first two ultra events.

More than anything else, I was able to show myself that I wouldn't be limited or defined by what had happened to me on that July morning. I also learned that you can't really separate your own determination from the love and support you receive from others—they're both essential.

Being a Marathon Maniac helped me to heal. 🐱

You Ponder Life While at Death's Door

by • Mike Brandt

Life is a journey full of adventures and memories, from inception to death. My goal in life is simple: to run a 5K when I am 100 years old.

My running has taken me to the far corners of the world: the Great Wall of China; the mud and glaciers of Antarctica; Arctic Bay on Baffin Island, 900 miles north of the Arctic Circle; the moais, guardians of Easter Island; the streets of London, historic Dublin, and around Red Square; the Sea of Galilee, the Tibetan Plateau, and the tip of South Africa; and the Inca Trail ending in Machu Picchu.

You begin to appreciate life when you are hospitalized for a severe heart attack or some other life-threatening event. Mine came on November 23, 2009, while on vacation with my wife outside Mexico City; we were touring the Aztec site known as Teotihuacan.

It was almost soundless, a slight, hot wind blowing across Avenida de Los Muertos (Avenue of the Dead), an eerie feeling from the twilight zone. After climbing to the top of the Pyramid of the Sun, some 250 feet, I took my moment of victory looking out over the valley. That is when I had my heart attack. Throughout the remainder of the day, I experienced different heart attack symptoms that finally subsided during the early evening.

At first, I did not suspect a heart attack. I had run marathons on all seven continents and 20 states and my 96th marathon just nine days before the heart attack, so the possibility of heart failure was the furthest thing from my mind.

My wife and I decided to cancel the remainder of the vacation and fly home. After landing in Sacramento 48 hours later, I went directly to the hospital, was admitted, and had quadruple-bypass surgery over Thanksgiving. As the nurses were prepping me for surgery, my thoughts were simply whether I was going to survive. Never having spent a night in the hospital, I was terrified not knowing whether I would wake up after the surgery and see my wife and family or even run another marathon.

I was released after 10 days and then faced the long road to recovery. The days that followed gave me time to ponder my extreme running adventures, wondering whether I would ever run again.

Recovery training was hard because of the circumstances, and the healing process dictated what I could or could not do. Since the heart attack, my adrenaline pushed me through the Rock 'n' Roll Marathon on June 6, 2010, just seven months after surgery. My next adventure will be the San Francisco Marathon and then Humpy's Classic Marathon in Anchorage, and my 100th marathon will be the Athens Marathon on October 31, 2010.

For a marathoner, it was a physical and mental struggle back, but with the support of my wife, family, friends, and fellow marathoners, I am running again and hope to for many years to come.

Postscript: *Mike successfully completed the 2010 Athens Marathon and went on to race in the 2011 Atacama Crossing in Chile.*

Priceless Pikes Peak

by • Peggy Shashy

After joining the Marathon Maniacs in April 2006, I decided to run the Pikes Peak Marathon. I was attempting to do all 50 states and decided that August would be a great time of year to visit Colorado. I invited friends to join me for a vacation there as well.

I bought a Landice Treadmill to train for hills and was given Matt Carpenter's book, *Training for the Ascent and Marathon on Pikes Peak*, as a training guide. It was hard to train on the "dreadmill," but I managed two to three and one-half hours at a time on it. To this day, I've never understood how I managed it. It was so boring.

When the weather was cool, I trained on the highest bridge in Jacksonville, Florida, since there are really no hills in Jacksonville. I got busted by the Florida Highway Patrol for running on the bridge. The patrolman was very kind and drove me all the way back to my car. He had been looking for me for a while, he said, and numerous calls had been placed that some crazy girl was running on the bridge. Well, what did he expect from a Maniac?

My training was going quite well until I ended up at the emergency room one morning less than four weeks before my marathon. I had had what I thought was the flu for several days, and even though I was drinking a lot of fluids, I got severely dehydrated. The doctor thought I had diverticulosis, but a CAT scan proved that other problems were apparent. I was given fluids and antibiotics and released from the hospital. I continued with problems for a week and was placed on antibiotics for six weeks. I had lost over 10 pounds. I was worried about the race and asked Maniac #3 for his advice about running it. He told me to do it if the doctors gave the OK.

But it was discovered on an ultrasound that I had an ovarian tumor and a smaller mass on my liver. The ovarian mass was suggestive of malignancy. I was devastated.

I thought that my life would be over if it was ovarian cancer. I had to run Pikes Peak because I thought that it might be the last race I would ever be able to do. I scheduled my surgery for the week after I got back from Colorado. It weighed heavily on my mind.

I arrived in Colorado two days before the race. I was still having gastro-intestinal problems but was drinking lots of fluids and eating bland diets. What I really wanted was an extra-large glass of wine, but I couldn't drink any alcohol with the medication I was prescribed.

A group of us decided to hike part of the Barr Trail up to around 9,000 feet. Some of our party didn't make it due to the altitude. The Pikes Peak Ascent of the marathon weekend had already begun, and several people were on the trail talking to us about altitude sickness. It made me very nervous. We also saw a few DNFs along the way. It was very sad. I worried that I would be one of them the following day.

On race day, I met up with another fellow Maniac and headed to the start. I was excited and nervous at the same time. This would prove to be one of the hardest races for me, both mentally and physically. Once the race started, I just focused on getting to the top. I took several pictures along the way and enjoyed numerous conversations along the course. And as always, there were lots of Maniacs introducing themselves as the ascent continued. Finally, I reached the Golden Stairs, and I was thrilled. It was cold up there, but the altitude was not causing any problems for me. I took some more pictures and hiked to the top. What a view it was! There is no way to describe how gorgeous it is at the top and to realize what it took to get there. Most people tell me they can barely drive to the top and stand there for any length of time without feeling the effects of the altitude. My ascent time was 4:57:32.

It was more treacherous descending the mountain. It was hard on my knees and difficult crawling over so many boulders. Once I made it down those few miles, I ran and never looked back. Finally, I got off the trail onto the roadway and realized that I was almost finished. It was a huge accom-

plishment for me, and I am grateful that I didn't once think about what was in store for me when I got back home. My finishing time was 8:31:01.

Our group headed to Rocky Mountain National Park the following day. We had a wonderful time and saw snow. There was abundant wildlife, and the scenery was beautiful. Every time I looked back at Pikes Peak, I could hardly believe that I had climbed that mountain. I will always remember that marathon as one of my favorites.

- Treadmill = $2,000
- Marathon, flights, hotels, and other costs = $1,000
- Finishing Pikes Peak and finding out that my ovarian tumor was benign = *priceless*

Being Pink in a Sea of Yellow

by • Robert López

"Hey, you're that guy who runs in pink!"

I get this a lot. It makes sense, really, because invariably somebody will say this while I'm running nearby in pink. Yes, I am the guy who runs in pink—well, one of the guys. I am not the guy who runs in a pink tutu; that fellow is Keith Straw from Philadelphia. He is faster than me. He also runs 100-milers. I do not, mostly because I can't count that high. But I do look good in pink.

I am an unabashed stunt runner. Stunt runners come in two overlapping flavors: (1) those who try to stand out by running in costumes and/or with props, and (2) those who put together, uh, colorful goals. Trying to qualify for Boston? Not a stunt run. Dude juggling while running a marathon backward? Stunt runner! Group trying to visit all the public library branches before they close? Stunt run!

Anyway, every stunt runner has a hook. Sometimes it is simply, "Dig me!" Other times, the hook involves a cause. My hook is that I run in pink with a big message handwritten on my back: *breast cancer sucks*. I know. Rather obvious message, eh? I started running in pink after my ex-wife was diagnosed with breast cancer, and I ditched my career temporarily to take care of her. She continues to battle through it; she is a warrior. I wanted to offer a tribute to her early on, and being a 10-star Maniac with 90 previous marathons, I knew a fun way. In January 2007, I bought a pink shirt (woman's XL; men's shirts don't come in pink) and a Sharpie. I traded the yellow singlet for the pink one with the slogan, and off I went to run 50-plus marathons in one year. I ended the year at 65.

A funny thing happened along the way. I started meeting people affected by cancer. I still do—lots of people. Usually, the conversation begins with that funny, obvious exclamation at the top of this story. Cancer survivors, family members and caregivers, relatives of folks who didn't make it, everybody has a story, and while these stories share certain themes, every story is unique.

My hook has changed; now, I pay tribute to everybody I meet, especially caregivers. This group is not given nearly enough credit. If you meet me, don't be surprised when I want to know about you and your connection to pink. Meeting folks and adding stories to the mix in my memory are why I still run in pink long after I finished number 65.

That said, I have an admission. I kind of like "dig me!" too. It is fun making people smile, and the pink helps— usually. Sometimes I question my choice. While running the Mississippi Blues Marathon (the 65th marathon to close out that string), I felt the special urge that strikes all marathoners. I was running through downtown Jackson and came across the Greyhound bus station. In I went to find the men's room. Hmm. It dawned on me that perhaps ducking into the bus-station bathroom wearing pink might not have been the wisest choice. I got several comments, which I shall not repeat here. I made it out alive, and I smile about it now. A pink-clad man surely has an interesting effect on nonrunners.

He has a different kind of effect on runners. While I get lots of well-wishers, a small number of runners seem to be less comfortable about a pink dude coming through. As I try to pass, runners surge so that I can't get in front more often than when I'm not wearing pink. And if Mr. Pink does pass, it is far more likely that the passee will try to immediately retake position and cut in front of me. I find this really interesting and usually quite hilarious. Some folks just don't want to be pinked.

I've been running in pink now for almost four years. Mostly, it has been very inspiring. It has definitely increased my worldview and expanded my empathy toward others. We all have similarities in many ways, but we are all definitely unique. The main thing I've learned through my experiences with cancer and stunt running in pink is simple: it's just running. Some training days are hard. Race days can be really hard. Injuries are, literally, a pain. I hear all the "secure in your masculinity" jokes over and over again. But I can't be overly serious about running when I look like kinetic bubble gum. My worst days running are *so* much easier than dealing with the shadow of cancer. It's just running.

By the way, when someone isn't pointing out that I'm the pink guy, the conversation sometimes starts with, "Hey, you are the guy running for breast cancer!"

Actually, I assure you that I'm firmly against it.

Musings of a Bangalore-Based Maniac

by • Bhasker Sharma

I stumbled across the Marathon Maniacs website in January 2006 when searching for marathon-related resources on the Internet. Marathon running in India was at a very early stage at that time, with the only event being the Mumbai Marathon, which was in its third year. I had run two marathons at that time. Marathon running in India started to gain momentum in 2007, which is when I set myself a goal of getting an entry into Marathon Maniacs, albeit at the bronze level.

I also mailed this information to the runners on *http://runnersforlife. com/*, the largest running community in this part of world. A lot of runners aspired to become part of Marathon Maniacs.

As was typical in India at that time, the first of the three marathons that I was planning to run in October got postponed. But I got lucky and travelled to New Jersey for work and was able to run the Suntrust Richmond Marathon in November 2007.

I saw quite a few Maniacs in that race—they were running in their MM gear—and that increased my determination to join the clan. I managed to

run my first ultramarathon at the first edition of the Bangalore Ultra on December 16, followed by the Mumbai Marathon on January 20, 2008. And I was extremely excited when I got a confirmation mail from Maniac #9, Marc, accepting my membership at the bronze level. I was a bit disappointed that I missed out on becoming the first MM from India; my good buddies Sunil Chainani and Vetcha Rajesh beat me to it. However, I was extremely thrilled to become Maniac #808, so much so that when I started a blog related to running in September 2008, I included my Maniac ID in the blog name.

Living in India and doing most of my running here meant that we Maniacs from India had few opportunities to interact with other maniacs in the US races. Therefore, I jumped at the opportunity to run again in the United States after becoming a part of the Marathon Maniacs. This was the Suntrust National Marathon in Washington, DC, on March 21, 2009. I looked out for MMs during this race and was extremely happy to interact with a couple of fellow Marathon Maniacs: Bekki, Maniac #244, running her 90th marathon; and Joseph, Maniac #381, running his 83rd. They both finished in 3:53. They wanted to know why I wasn't running in Maniac gear. Inspired by the few minutes of running with them, I managed to get a PR, finishing below four hours for the first time.

There are only four MMs from India, but I am happy to state that running as a sport has come a long way in India over the last few years. We now have at least five full marathons or ultras each year.

Though I have now obtained my MM T-shirt, I have not had an opportunity to wear it in a race in the United States yet. Even though I do not get to meet and interact with MMs often enough, I consider myself an MM "lifer" and look forward to upgrading myself from the bronze level at some point in the future. And I visit the website at least every time I complete a marathon or an ultra in order to enter my race there!

Postscript: *In the last 12 months, Bhasker ran his longest distance of 75K at the fourth Bangalore Ultra and finished first overall out of the 17 runners who completed the run. He also did his best marathon finish at his sixth consecutive Mumbai Marathon in January 2011, with a time of 3:53. Bhasker is also an active member of a running group called BHUKMP formed by a bunch of runners aspiring to run each of the six marathons and ultramarathons that are run in India every year (Bangalore Midnight Marathon, Hyderabad Marathon, Bangalore Ultramarathon, Kaveri Trail Marathon, Mumbai Marathon, and Pondicherry Marathon).* 🐾

One Night, One Marathon: Bangkok

by • Ingrid Peterson

It's 1:00 A.M. Taxis appear from all directions, dropping off runners into the dark near the Grand Palace for the Bangkok Marathon. Many runners have lined up for prerace massages of menthol, oil of eucalyptus, and wintergreen. The pungent smell permeates the 80-degree temperature and humidity. Dozens of tables sag under bananas piled 3 feet high. Volunteers sleep underneath. Lines are long for the porta-potty buses. The instructions are in Thai.

The marathon begins. Runners disappear into the darkness. I can follow their mentholated scent and their bright-yellow singlets that reflect what light there is.

Crossing the bridges leading out of Bangkok, the streetlamps light the road at intervals, rarely bright enough to check your watch by. The dark forms of photographers startle you when they step out of the shadows. A bike passes occasionally.

Except for runners' footsteps, there is mostly silence, but suddenly, there is a crescendo of noise. The leaders are passing, going in the opposite direction. There is just enough time to jump out of the path of the wheelchair athletes. Soon after the first runner, a single-file line of 14 African runners emerges. One by one, a slender form appears under a streetlamp, only to be swallowed again by darkness. They seem to float. As quickly as they came, they are gone.

I notice that I am running alone. I wonder whether it is because of my fuel belt. There are four red bottles and a bulging pouch with iPod wires hanging down. It looks as if I might detonate. No one else wears a fuel belt. No one else wears a skirt, either.

The first and only porta-potty bus looms up out of the darkness, its dark-gray bulk spitting out runners as I pass. I can wait.

The course descends into the even greater darkness of the city. Here the road is rougher and traffic becomes an issue at intersections. Shadowy vendors are setting up their sidewalk food stands for the day. They take no notice of runners who won't be buying.

In the darkness, I can smell that we are passing the zoo.

Next we go past three sides of the moat-enclosed King's Palace. I think of the large Komodo dragons that live in the moat and hope that they sleep at night. I see many armed guards. Are they for the king, or the dragons, or to protect us from the demonstrators camped out nearby? I am too tired to worry about it.

We run near the Government House, but our way is blocked. We are rerouted. The demonstrators have been throwing pipe bombs and Molotov cocktails again. Dawn has come. There is a 2-baht coin on the ground. It's worth 5 cents. I bend to pick it up but am too stiff. I walk on. Someone runs up behind me. "You dropped this." He hands me the coin and runs on. His challenge is met. I run past him with a thank you in Thai and finish the race. 🐱

The Twisted Ankle Trail Marathon

by • Jason Rogers

The marathon where I qualified to join Marathon Maniacs was also the event that kicked off my enthusiasm for trail running. After completing my first two marathons—the Snickers Marathon Energy Bar Marathon in Albany, Georgia, on March 7, 2009, and the ING Georgia Marathon in Atlanta, Georgia, on March 29, 2009—I decided to attempt the Twisted Ankle Trail Marathon on May 16. It is held at a state park in Summerville, Georgia, and aside from the foreboding name, the race is known for a brutal 700-foot ascent in less than a half mile at mile three, beautiful stretches of ridge trail at the top of the ascent, and its lack of finisher's medals. Makeshift medals are given to age-group winners, but most finishers receive only a T-shirt. The fact that the Twisted Ankle Trail Marathon starts at 9:00 A.M. in mid-May adds to its reputation as a challenging event.

After dealing with crowded road corrals at the start of my previous marathon, I was pleasantly surprised by the low-key start at the Twisted Ankle Trail Marathon. The race director stood on a picnic table to give a few words of motivation to the crowd of 300 or so runners standing around and then sent us off.

After a fairly flat two-mile run around a campground lake, I started the brutal ascent up Becky's Bluff, the sharp climb named after the race director. You know that you're in for an interesting marathon experience when you can almost reach out with your hand and touch the same hill that you are climbing! Several runners were using trees to pull themselves up the ascent. I passed people who were resting by leaning against tree trunks. Fortunately, we were rewarded at the top by an aid-station table full of peanut butter and jelly sandwiches, Gummi Bears, M&M's, and orange slices. I quickly learned that trail marathons easily outdo the road marathons in terms of aid-station food.

At the top of this climb, I split from the half-marathoners and found myself coasting along a beautiful single-track trail on the ridge with no other runners in sight. This was the moment when I realized the strange appeal of trail races.

I love cheering roadside crowds as much as the next person, but there is something about running by myself through a scenic wooded area that sets me at ease and takes the pressure off about the distance that I must conquer. I thought of the Robert Frost line, "The woods are lovely, dark, and deep, but I have promises to keep, and miles to go before I sleep."

Two more challenging climbs, a steep downhill ascent, and a final campground circle later, I was finally running over a lake on a wooden boardwalk to a small cheering crowd at the finish line, where I completed my third marathon in three months and became the Marathon Maniac that I am. I've since completed two more trail marathons and four trail ultramarathons.

I didn't twist my ankle at the Twisted Ankle Trail Marathon, but I might have twisted my brain.

The 2010 Mount Si 50-Mile Ultra

by • Mike Kuhlmann

The sun was finally warming the southern slopes of the cascade foothills as I left the Rattlesnake Lake aid station for the second time. The first visit was about two hours before when I retrieved my drop bag to eat an energy bar, refilled my water bottle with my own special energy elixir, and reapplied Bodyglide to areas prone to chafing. Surprisingly, my feet were still in good shape—no blisters, no hot spots, no need for duct tape. I had been running now for 8 hours, 30 minutes. During the last 10 miles, my calf muscles were threatening to cramp anytime I tried to increase my pace beyond a shuffle. I hoped that the two electrolyte tablets—the ninth and 10th taken today—would curb the cramping.

The trail is well maintained and consists of hard-packed gravel but with just enough sticks, rocks, and potholes to cause tripping if your eyes or mind wandered too far. I'm having second thoughts about not wearing my gaiters. I'm certain that I have a small rock or piece of bark in my left shoe, but unless it starts chewing on my foot, I'm not willing to stop. Previous experience in trying to remove a shoe this late in a race resulted in muscle cramping that kept me hopping on one foot for 10 minutes before I could get the shoe back on. Today is not the day, and this is not the course, to start running barefoot.

Good; whatever is in my shoe has moved to the front of my toes and has found a resting place away from my foot. Off to my left, a warning sign reads "Bears and mountain lions recently spotted in this area."

It's not exactly the motivational message I'm looking for. I've heard it said, "You don't need to be able to outrun a bear or a cougar, you just need to be faster than the person you're with."

Today, I am pretty sure that almost all runners have, or can, outrun me. Oh, I remember passing one or two racers a while ago, and every five to 10 minutes one of the relay-team members flies by; but from a predator's perspective, I am likely a slow-moving meal. I can only hope that they're napping in the sun and don't want to expend the energy or that they are downwind of my runner's eight-hour stink and it offends their senses. Just keep moving. At least the warmth of the early-afternoon sun feels good on my back.

When the race started at 6:00 A.M., the temperature was below zero; frost formed on several runners' stocking caps as we started. During the first few miles, the rhythmic, visible breath of the 50-plus runners declared in each that there was a little engine that could. It was an inspiration to be part of this group, but I also knew that most would soon outpace me and that I would run much of the time alone. I would get to see the leaders and the rest of the runners, including my youngest daughter (MM #761) twice, as there were two out-and-back sections to the course.

The leader's pace is phenomenal. The first time I see Ryne Melcher coming, I'm at about mile eight and he is at about mile 12. I'm thinking that one of the relay teams has started early. But as he runs toward me, his bib color and number identify him as a solo ultrarunner. I see him again several hours later when I'm at about mile 25 and he is at mile 45. He is still maintaining the same pace. Ryne goes on to win the race, averaging a pace of just over 7 minutes per mile. He will end up finishing the race as I'm just leaving the Rattlesnake Lake aid station for the first time.

While he's come to race, I've come to finish.

The official cutoff time for this race was advertised as 5:00 P.M., which was 11 hours, start to finish. At this point, I've got a little over two hours to make this official.

I feel anguish for my daughter. At 25 miles, her hamstrings were tightening up, and by 30 miles, she was noticeably adjusting her stride to compensate. She didn't want to risk injury this early in the season and decided to drop out, a DNF. Her day ended as a 30-mile training run. She made a difficult but prudent decision since we were registered to run four marathons in the next eight weeks. She was the reason I was out here running.

As I'm running, I recall how it all started. My wife and I crewed for her first marathon in 2006. I remembered sitting with her before the start of the race, listening to the runners and feeling their excitement. They were all connected by the common cause to successfully complete the 26.2-mile course in front of them.

I noticed that there was extra energy around a group of runners, each wearing a yellow singlet with the caricature of a crazed runner with a cat on his head. I was not sure what they were about, but they really seemed to be enjoying themselves. My daughter told me they were members of a running club called "Marathon Nuts, Crazies, or something." She also told me that to get into the club you had to run something like three marathons in three months or two marathons in two weeks. As a sane person, I knew that was not possible and that she had to be mistaken. During the race, I saw the front of the singlet that identified the club as "Marathon Maniacs."

At the end of my daughter's first marathon, as we were waiting for her to receive an age-group award, we were sitting close enough to overhear the conversation of two club members. They were talking about a recently completed "double"—running a marathon on two consecutive days. I was sure that I had misunderstood what they were talking about or that they were a little crazed from just running a marathon. I remembered their faces and later learned the two were MM #1 and MM #3.

Eighteen months later, I was admitted into the asylum as MM #678. Twenty months later, my younger daughter was admitted as MM #761. My older daughter was satisfied running an occasional half-marathon and thought we were nuts for running 26.2 miles. Then she witnessed the 2008 Tacoma City Marathon, sponsored and attended by over a hundred MMs. She was smitten. Even though she had never run a marathon, she registered to run three marathons in three months to attempt qualification for MM membership. She entered the asylum in September 2008 as MM #1011. We all signed up to run 2010 marathons in Tacoma, Olympia, and . . .

Movement off the left side of the trail!

All my senses are on full alert.

I can hear a runner coming up fast behind me—at least, it sounds like a runner.

Screams just behind me!

As I begin to turn around, a young female runner jumps into my arms screaming, "Snakes! I hate snakes!"

I respond, "Thank God! I thought it was a cougar or I was hallucinating. Snakes are bad but better than the alternatives."

She was down the trail before I ended my response. I guess she decided that snakes were preferable to hugging some old guy wearing an eight-hour-and-45-minute running stink.

Apparently, the movement I just saw and what caused the reaction from the female relay runner were several snakes slithering off the sun-bathed trail to keep from getting trampled underfoot. Well, that adds a little excitement and recharges me for the last couple of hours of this race.

Nine hours and 20 minutes into this race, I regret not bringing another water bottle. I have about 2 ounces of my special mix left but really need a drink of water to wash down my last two electrolyte tablets.

I should be approaching an unmanned aid station soon.

I can see it—a table with several 5-gallon containers of water.

All empty! Not good! Another mile to the team relay exchange point. I hope to find water there. It's a long, slow mile.

I must look parched, because as I approach the exchange point, people point me to the water containers without my uttering a sound.

Twelve to 14 ounces later, I'm back on the trail to finish the last few miles. As I move through the last miles, my confidence grows—I think I'll finish under the cutoff time with a 12- to 15-minute margin.

The last miles are almost always special but today more than most. My emotions begin to surface, and tears fill my eyes. My concrete legs lighten and loosen up. The shuffle increases to a jog, and then with about one mile remaining, I'm actually running. There are tears rolling down my cheeks as I turn the corner and see the finish, now only about 200 meters away.

I'm going to finish it—my first 50-mile race—with a little time to spare. My daughter and wife are about 100 meters from the finish. They cheer me on. They tell me later that they're also amazed that I'm still upright. The race director meets me just after I cross the finish line and presents the finisher's medal. He congratulates me with a warm, sincere handshake, some kind words, and a pat on the shoulder.

Forty-eight runners finish the 50 mile-race. The fastest male, Ryne Melcher, finishes in 5:54:15 (a course record). The fastest female, Jody Aslett, finishes in 7:34:10. I finish well off the winning pace in 10:42:32—just 17-plus minutes under the official cutoff time.

But for me, it has been a good day—no injuries, no chafing, no blisters, no medical attention required. I had only one more obstacle: getting out of the car when I got home.

35

Making Maniacs at the Flat Ass

by • Rob Roy Smith

My friend and running partner, Hoa Pham-Schober, and I became Marathon Maniacs on a cold, very wet day in December 2007. The idea of becoming a Maniac hatched innocently enough. Hoa and I have two weaknesses: running and being easily persuaded by the other to run races. We had signed up for the Las Vegas Marathon in December 2007, which would have been my first, when we decided that it would be a good idea for me to run a "warm-up" marathon in Portland, Oregon, in October 2007. That race went well, if my rocking and crying softly while wrapped in a space blanket at the end of the race signifies a good marathon.

Realizing that running Portland and Las Vegas within three months put us within reach of becoming Maniacs, it took very little persuasion for us to sign up for the Pigtails Flat Ass Ultra, an out-and-back 50K on a trail south of Seattle on December 22, 2007. It would give us our three marathons in three months. Frankly, I am not sure which of these ideas sounded crazier: a 50K two weeks after running a marathon or running a 50K three days before Christmas on the day my mother arrived from New Jersey to spend the holiday with me. Putting these and all other rational concerns behind us, Hoa and I lined up with 67 other hardy souls at daybreak in 30-degree weather to take on the course. Within minutes, it started to rain.

Within hours, it began to pour, and there was nothing to be done other than splash to a finish. At mile 22, my future wife—who may have suffered more than the runners by having the misfortune of providing race support on her road bike—came alongside and asked how I was doing. I begged her to let me on the bike. She wisely refused, and I plodded along, watching the miles tick by ever more slowly on my GPS. After 5 hours and 14 minutes, I crossed the finish line with Hoa not far behind, having completed our first ultra and becoming Maniacs.

We were elated (and very hungry). The finisher's medal was a pink Styrofoam pig. It is with great pride that I told everyone that holiday that I ran over 31 miles for a Styrofoam pig on a ribbon. Few understood the significance, and many questioned my sanity. But becoming a Maniac was a wonderful experience. It continues to be. The encouragement from all those yellow-singlet-clad racers at marathons since 2007 has been an inspiration to me in every marathon since.

Millennial Dragon—The Great Wall Marathon

Excerpts.

by • Rodolfo Lucena

Pools of new, dense, red blood screamed the warning: You can't be too careful on the steps of the Great Wall. But we went on running through pure gut instinct on the greatest construction ever made.

There are more than 6,000 kilometers of fortress mounted on mountain crests, protecting the ancient Chinese dynasties from attacks from the northern barbarians. Only a small part of the wall is reserved for those of us who take part in the Great Wall of China Marathon, free of tourists and full of challenges: more than 1,700 steps of various sizes, partially decayed areas, and portions that were in danger of collapsing.

At three o'clock in the morning of May 22, Eleonora, my wife, and I got onto the bus that would take us to the starting point of the competition, about a three-hour trip northeast from Beijing. Altogether, more than two dozen buses left Beijing hotels, bringing runners from 30 countries to the starting point.

When we arrived at the starting point in Huangyaguan, in the province of Tianjin, it was about 6:30 A.M. It was mighty cold and cloudy, but the forecast was for 30 degrees Celsius, as it had been the day before.

The wind died down, and we were able to stand still without shivering in the little fortified citadel from which we were about to leave to confront the Millennial Dragon (a nickname for the Great Wall of China). We were on flatlands where perhaps in ancient times armies would gather, a small village protected by the wall. Today, the closed-in area is divided into various segments, including a large parking lot surrounded by small tourist shops, stalls, and camels (by paying a modest amount of money, you can mount and have your picture taken on one) and the Yin Yang Square, where local civic and sports events take place. It takes its name from the Taoist masculine and feminine signs that decorate the center of the square.

Fewer than 500 people would be confronting various distances, from the complete course of the marathon to a smaller version of 10 kilometers, all including parts of the wall.

When we started to climb the hill that would get us to the wall, I couldn't hold back my enthusiasm anymore. Some of the runners were really enjoying themselves: one couple had a hard time going up face first and later trotted backward, uphill, offering energy candies to the slower ones.

A light breeze made the heat of the sun more bearable, especially since all those early-morning clouds had disappeared and the sun was shining brightly. Just before the five-kilometer mark, there were two water stops placed in strategic locations. Our work was rewarded when we finally caught the view of a small gate on which iron plaques announced the entrance to the Great Wall. I was meeting up with history.

The Great Wall of China was built by thousands of workers over the centuries. Most of the Great Wall that remains today was built during the Ming Dynasty (1368–1644). Some of the earliest remains date back to the Warring States Period (476 BC–221 BC), which is the portion that we're running through.

Some say that if you built a wall from the bricks and stones used for this fortress, it would be 2 1/2 meters high and 1 meter wide, reaching around the circumference of the earth at the equator.

There are questions about whether a wall can protect the population. The Mongols, for example, came from the north and took over the country. They were conquered by the Mings, whose dynasty lasted almost 300 years but who were deposed by enemies coming from the other side of the wall, the Manchus.

The first stairs we encountered were wonderful, with steps made of gray bricks. The places where we came down that were steeper were marked with white paint. However, no one warned us that, although they were of equal size, the steps were not of equal height. It was a good thing that, two days before, we made a scouting trip, walking lightly and carefully on all the area of the fortress. I said to myself, *The easiest parts are also the most dangerous; I can't take anything for granted; I shouldn't get too excited; each step is a step.*

It was pretty easy until we arrived at the tower marking the highest point of the track over the wall. After that, the trail is made of fieldstone and irregular-sized rocks. The trail gets narrower, the way down gets steeper, and in some parts, there are no walls. More stones, another passageway, one more tower, and finally on top, I have the view of the town that we started from. I can't believe that we have to go back down there. But it's true. A small track without steps allows us to trot, and just as it seems that we have to face another monstrous uphill climb, people from the organization let us know that we need to break off to the right, a set of stairs, and we are off the wall.

From the wall, we got off the mountain quickly, going down a trail cut into the earth, on ground covered with frightening gravel that made me worry about sliding at any moment. There is a lot going on, and you need to really concentrate, because in one small curve, your foot can just go. We kept catching sight of the town, and I hoped to see Eleonora. Once in a while, I waved to the people below. Who knows, maybe she saw me.

"Rodooooolfo." I heard my name being called from far away, from the other side of the dry riverbed—Eleonora, armed with her camera. I blew her kisses and "I love yous," and then yelled, "It's all downhill from here!" and left the mountain, returning to the wall that surrounded the town of Huangyaguan.

I finally arrived at the small village where we would start our reentry to the wall. It was at the 34th kilometer mark that the truth about this race finally revealed itself.

We would have to climb the mountain through the most difficult path. The stairs carved into the rocks were slippery and treacherous. With each step, your leg went up 40 centimeters, 50 on another. You climbed, you stopped, you looked at the next challenge, and you put out your foot again. My quadriceps screamed with each step, asking for another rest.

Resting and climbing, I finally got back to the mountain top and to the entrance of the Great Wall. This track wasn't exactly refreshing, but it was a little less savage than the stone-paved track. I could see other runners; I could stop and rest. Many people sat on the steps, where the vendors took advantage of the situation and offered them regional fruit, principally a kind of pear, very white but tasteless, from what they told me.

I came into the town yelling, "Brazil," "Brazil," shouted my love for Eleonora, and when I saw the finish line, I opened my arms to make myself into a small airplane. It was only then that I saw Eleonora. She was in front of me, on the other side of the finish line, taking pictures without stop. The camera didn't leave her face, but I'm getting there, I'm coming with my lips already puckered—take away the camera and get my kiss. I ran 6 hours, 54 minutes, 2 seconds. In the bleachers, what's left of the public laughs and applauds. It's party time at the Yin Yang Square.

Bib 168

by • Valentine-John Ridao

Two weeks before the 2007 Leavenworth Marathon in Washington, a double-loop race that coincides with Oktoberfest, my training program hit the wall. I hurt my back and caught a nasty cold.

The cold bug was still in my chest when I was driving to the start line for the Leavenworth Marathon with my future wife, Regina. I told her that maybe I should run the half-marathon instead and call it good.

It was just a passing thought.

We arrived in time, and before the race began I saw two familiar faces: Leslie Miller (MM #294) and Bob Dolphin (MM #32). Bob and Lenore Dolphin are my marathon parents since my introduction to the marathon was at their race in 2007, the Yakima River Canyon Marathon.

The air was nippy as the race began, and many of the locals had their fireplaces going. The smoke added to the challenging workout that my lungs were about to receive.

As I was completing the first loop and coming upon the start/finish area, I told myself that it would be OK to quit while I was still alive and in love. However, I could delay my decision to quit or continue since I would have to pass the start/finish area one more time before heading out for the bulk of the second loop. I ran past the start/finish area for my second loop, determined that there was no turning back.

It was a long and difficult journey. After about 22 miles, I was in last place! Running through a park, I came upon some Korean tourists. I greeted them with "an-nyung-ha-se-yo," which means "hello." I knew that I looked terrible and tried to gain some sympathy by offering to sell them my sweaty visor for $5 if they would agree to finish the race for me. No takers. It was lonely. I was trying everything to keep myself company.

As I raced to the finish line, I saw Regina and Bob and Lenore Dolphin waiting for me. I marched to Lenore and told her in a military fashion: "All runners accounted for." Bob told me that, except in an emergency, it's always better to finish than to DNF. He was right. I will always have empathy for all last-place finishers and cheer them on for finishing the race and not letting the race finish them.

Sometime during the last mile, I got intimately acquainted with my bib—bib 168—and made a connection between it and my 2007 Leavenworth Marathon experience One: I did not finish first. Six: It would take me at least six hours to finish. Eight: This was my eighth marathon. Bib numbers come and go, but bib 168 from my 2007 Leavenworth Marathon will always be special to me. And thanks for waiting for me, Regina.

The Walls
Come Down

by • Mike Moore

Many of us who are Marathon Maniacs are asked, "How did you become a Maniac?" and, "Why do you run so many marathons?" Many times our answers sound the same. The accomplishment of running a marathon, whether as an elite or in the middle of the pack or simply as a finisher, is a special goal, although we seem to have similar stories behind our drive to excel.

The marathon is unique in a way because it is not unique; all it takes is shoes and the will to finish. In a way, it is the most egalitarian of sports. It is a sports accomplishment that everyone can reach, and in the end, each marathon really is not a race against others, it is a race against ourselves.

And that's why my story is special to me. Like many other military couples, my wife and I had some really difficult times when I got back from my longest tour in Iraq. Except for a two-week break in about the middle of my tour, I was gone for 17 months. My daughter had not reached her second birthday when I left; she was 4 when I returned. As a family, we had to start over, and the way we did that, starting with my wife and me, was to run.

We ran with a jogging stroller through the streets near our home in Tacoma and then finally on our own through one, then two half-marathons. I know that my wife enjoyed running with me, spending time with me while doing something I loved to do, but I knew that there was a little bit missing, something that I could not put my finger on. There seemed to be a barrier between us.

Finally, we shared a marathon. We ran at Walt Disney World together in 2008. I ran with her as part of my third Goofy Challenge, running the marathon after the half-marathon the day before.

We started off strong, a good solid pace. It was hotter than we expected, and my wife had to contend with the usual first-time marathoner's trials and drama: the blisters, the cramps, and then the despair. Finally, at mile 20, knowing that I would not finish the Goofy Challenge without finishing the marathon successfully, she told me to go on without her. I touched her arm and told her, "If you don't finish, I don't finish. I don't want to be at the finish line without you."

At that moment, something clicked. The walls came down. Instead of two people "working out our differences," we were a team, a couple, a family. When the race was finished and we were getting on the flight home, I took our children down the aisle to our seats. My wife was stopped by an elderly woman at the front of the plane who saw her with her medal and asked her, "Are you a marathoner?" and she looked at me and smiled and said, "Yes, ma'am, I am."

Triumph Over Adversity: My Five-Star Quest

by • Valerie Merges

The wind gust stopped my forward momentum. As my knee rose for the next step, the force of the air blast prevented my leg from advancing. My progress was halted midstep, resulting in a moment where I was frozen midstride. It took enormous effort to push my leg against the powerful, gusting wind.

Struggling to advance, I leaned sharply forward. Under normal conditions, this forward tilt would result in a face plant. But out here, battling against the squalls of pelting rain, forward momentum was critical. It was too cold to stop.

The Bear Lake Marathon is normally a scenic course around an 18-mile-long lake straddling the Utah-Idaho border. Bear Lake has a distinctive turquoise-blue color, the result of suspended limestone deposits in the water. The lake is bordered by the Bear River Mountains, which create a picturesque contrast to the vast lake surface. In previous years, marathon participants complained about the 80-degree temperatures. This year the windchill may put the temperature below freezing.

If I successfully complete this race, it will give me my five stars—the ruthenium level!

The horizontal rain stings my face. Squinting, I see a mile marker ahead. My legs are sluggish; they don't respond to my brain's command to speed up so I can read the sign. The wind takes my hat for the third time; I give up and grab the hat with my frozen right hand. The mesh hat was useless, anyway; rain had long ago saturated my hair. The fuzzy number come into view—"13." I'm only halfway! For the first time running a marathon, I'm not sure I can make it.

The start of the race was warm enough that one runner opted to run without a shirt. Advertised as a "50-state special," this event offered a rare combination of Friday/Saturday, two-state, back-to-back marathons. As a result, the race had attracted Maniacs, 50 staters, and a few locals.

There were only two busloads of runners set to begin running Saturday morning (the second day of running). Not only did this low-key race lack the normal drop-bag procedures or timing chips, there wasn't even a starting line drawn on the street. We stood in the road cracking jokes behind the imaginary timing mat while the race director waited for the porta-potties to empty. During the countdown, I noticed that we would be running toward an area of dark clouds. At 6,000 feet elevation, wouldn't the clouds naturally look more menacing?

The horn sounded, and we began running alongside Bear Lake. The small group of runners quickly spread out along the road. What a contrast from last weekend at the San Diego Rock 'n' Roll Marathon, where there were 30,000 runners at the start line. Since this was not my first back-to-back marathon, I relaxed into a slow pace. I knew that the best strategy was to conserve energy at the outset and save it for the last half of the run. How thankful I would be later in the race that I still had some energy in reserve.

Shortly after passing mile-marker 13, the course took a 90-degree turn. Normally this two-mile stretch of dirt road is a pleasant change from pounding the tarmac. Today, however, it was transformed into two miles of mud puddles. My foot sank into muck with each step and then slipped precariously as I pushed off my toes. There was no avoiding the pooling water. When the noise of the wind waned, I could hear my feet: "kersplash, kersplash."

This was my first marathon without an iPod (I didn't want to ruin it in the rain). Whether it was the lack of headphones or the slower pace, I had been able to converse with fellow runners during the first few miles of the race. I was amazed to hear stories of extreme dedication. After back-to-back marathons, one Maniac would be driving overnight to Colorado (to make a triple). Then there was Bob from Long Island, who was staying in a tent at the KOA campground. But once the storm hit, there was no more conversation. It was too much effort to shout over the wind noise. It was too much effort to *listen* to someone shouting over the wind noise. We were all on our own now; we all had our own personal struggle against the elements.

My personal struggle was with hypothermia. With my socks saturated, my feet began sloshing in my shoes. My thin gloves did little to keep my hands warm; my fingers stung with the cold. My matted ponytail was dripping down the back of my neck. My clothes were saturated. And there were 12 more miles to go.

Thankfully, there was no warm sag wagon behind me, tempting me to DNF. There is no chance for a PB, zero possibility of a BQ. I briefly considered knocking on the door of one of the farmhouses. I imagined myself saying, "Could I just warm up in your house for a few minutes? Do you have any hot drinks?" But would I become even more hypothermic if I stopped? I had better keep moving. Faster is better. Running is warmer.

I looked up to see headlights coming toward me. I moved toward the side of the muddy road. The headlights are advancing quickly; why won't the driver slow down? Perhaps my low visibility is a factor. Wearing black from head to toe is a bad strategy on an open course during a rainstorm. I bet the driver can't see me between swipes of his windshield wipers. I move to the extreme edge of the road as the car speeds by—spraying me with mud. *No problem,* I think. *I'm sure the rain will give me a complete rinse by the time I cross the finish line.*

The next turn comes into view—a major road, a paved road, a very *recently* paved black-asphalt road. As I make the turn, I see that the road is so recently paved that it has no painted lines on the side. My black outfit will render me undetectable to motorists: great for a ninja but not so great for my chances of finishing this marathon. I attempt to increase my pace out of fear for my safety.

Only 10 more miles.

The rain begins to subside. I experience the onset of searing pain in my feet. My toes have become numb from the cold but are now thawing out. The pain intensifies; I'm forced to slow to a walk. I think about a running friend who I called "Ponytail." She told me about her tight schedule to obtain titanium level, but this morning she was suffering from plantar fasciitis. I wonder if she's ahead of me on the course or behind me somewhere. Anyone who has to walk this course is experiencing increased suffering from the longer duration spent in the cold and rain.

I'm walking against traffic. Up ahead, I see a semitruck heading toward me. I must be invisible. The driver does not see me; the truck is not moving over. As the semi looms closer, I see why. A car is passing the truck on the opposite side of the road. I stumble down the embankment to protect myself as the truck sprays me with road grease. Only nine more miles.

My run has turned into an epic slog. It's punctuated by moments of danger. The normally beautiful-blue Bear Lake appears gray with foaming whitecaps. For two days of running, this lake has been on my right side. Both races turn clockwise around the lake until the runners have circumnavigated 52.4 miles. Glancing at the lake today has not had a calming effect. No, watching the rolling waves seems to intensify the feeling of aloneness. It's me against the elements.

I battle onward. The miles slowly tick off. That tremendous feeling begins to well up: I know that I can make it! Two more miles; I transition into a fast shuffle. I catch four walkers and give them the infamous "almost there!" encouragement. I can see flashing police lights ahead. That must mean the finish line is within sight.

I pick up my pace, heading toward the flashing light. Where is the finish line? Oh, no, the police are only helping me to cross the road. I'm crushed; this is my finish line sprint, and I can't hold it much longer. I have to make a 90-degree turn and then run some more! But at least I can finally see the archway for the finish.

There are no cheering spectators, no racers milling about with medals around their neck, none of the usual postrace crowds. I'm handed my finish medal, and I'm done. I'm torn between feelings of relief—it's over—and euphoria—*five stars*!

It was an unusually hard effort that brought me to the next level of Marathon Maniacness. Five stars, everybody. *Five stars*!

The general public can't comprehend the accomplishment. After all, don't we label it "The Insane Asylum?" Although I'm cold and wet, I'm riding the wave of postrace euphoria.

Postscript: *Valerie went on to complete her first 50-mile race in 2011. She hopes to obtain the coveted six stars while training for her next goal, a 100-mile event.*

Being a Maniac

by • Dean Schuster

I am now a card-carrying member of a noted progressive organization. My group is dedicated to running marathons, lots of them. It's not exactly a lofty proposition, but we can't take ourselves seriously every minute, can we?

Certainly, this group does not. These are the Marathon Maniacs. I'm number 540. The Maniacs organized in 2003 when several extremely motivated runners decided to codify their marathon addiction. I day, this can mean dozens of mara-

thons annually. Maniac #1 recently completed a Heinz special—57 marathons in one year. The frequent-flyer implications alone boggle the mind.

If you've run a marathon recently, you may have seen a Maniac, easily identifiable by the shocking-yellow singlet. They are far from shy. Clearly, this is a society for people with way too much free time and an oddball itch to fill it with rigorous aerobic exercise.

And they're deliciously irreverent. You have to love an organization whose spasmodic-runner logo (reminiscent of Robert Crumb) comes complete with an extremely distressed black cat perched on his head. The whole thing conjures up images of obsessively compulsive runners jaunting along, iPods set to Enigma's quasi-hip-hop Gregorian chants—not that there's anything wrong with that.

Of course, the Maniacs don't just run marathons, they keep score. Members track their conquests on a bare-knuckles website. There, in the Insane Asylum, marathons are tracked by number, location, and frequency.

One thing is certain: those who run the most marathons are rated highest. Membership levels are named mostly after elements of the periodic table. The rarer the element, the more difficult the requirement to achieve it. In a nod to grammar-school reward charts, stars denote level. The more stars, the better.

The rating system does, however, get points for style. The delightfully obscure iridium level (four stars) requires 19 to 25 marathons in one year. Up the chain, the osmium level (six stars) can be reached if you finish six marathons in 16 days. The highest level, titanium, boasts 10 stars and requires 52 marathons in one year. I can just see the Maniacs now, bad dubbing and all, "Your ruthenium kung fu is strong, but my palladium cannot be defeated!"

I must bow to such achievement. You see, I'm just a bronze Maniac.

Bronze is not even an element. It's just a measly alloy, the only one on the list. For this lowest of all levels (one star), I ran two marathons in eight days, squeaking in by the skin of my plebeian teeth.

I guess this means that at Marathon Maniac conventions, I'll be the guy handing out towels in the restroom.

Hey, I just work here; I'm MM #540.

How to Get to the Iridium Level of Marathon Maniacs on the Cheap While Serving the Runner

by • George Rehmet

Many races and running clubs fall under the umbrella of the national organization of the Road Runners Club of America (RRCA). To reach out to these clubs and runners, the RRCA has state representatives who volunteer their time. I'm the Coastal California State Representative. In late 2007, I was called upon to take up a challenging task—to direct a national convention for the RRCA in 2009 in San Francisco.

Besides overseeing the many activities of putting on a convention, I had to promote the convention. I knew that I needed a running goal to keep my sanity. My goal was to run 12 marathons or ultras in a year with the other goal of joining Marathon Maniacs at the iridium level by running marathons in nine states. But I needed to do it on the cheap. Here is what I did for each state:

1. **Little Rock Marathon**—took a little detour after an educational conference in Chicago. Most of my airfare paid for.

2. **Flying Pig Marathon**—national RRCA convention was there. All expenses paid. Yes!

3. **Casper Marathon**—having frequent-flyer miles for United, I look for the most expensive destination that has a marathon that I can fly to for free. Wyoming was the winner, plus the rooms were inexpensive.

4. **Montana Marathon**—at the RRCA convention, there is an auction. I scored a free entry and room for this race for $25. Just had to pay for airfare. Luckily, Montana's state representative drove me around.

5. **Tahoe Rim Trail 50 K**—Nevada's state representative invited me to run this race, which he directs, for free. The race was a four-hour drive from my home in Daly City. I used my priority rewards to get free hotel nights. The altitude got to me.

6. **New York City Marathon**—I had to suck up the costs for this one. I qualified for the race so there was no way I was going to miss a chance to run there.

7. **Grand Canyon Marathon**—another conference in Phoenix, Arizona, so free airfare. I just had to arrive a couple of days before and drive up. Slept in my car since I did not see the need for a hotel room at the race site for five hours.

8. **Rocket City Marathon**—I used the stay-with-the-relatives trick. We made a weekend of driving to Huntsville, Alabama, from Nashville.

9. **For California**, I did the Diablo Marathon, Oakland's Lake Merritt Six-Hour Race, the Headlands 50, and the San Francisco 12-Hour Race. I did these races as part of a series in which I placed second overall. Sweet!

Postscript: *Mission accomplished! George was able to promote the convention at most of these places. The RRCA Convention in San Francisco proved to be wildly successful. George was also selected as the Outstanding RRCA State Representative.*

The Oldest Marathon Maniacs

by • Lenore Dolphin

Who would get married on a Wednesday night so as not to interfere with the groom's weekend races? The answer seems logical that it must be someone with Marathon Maniac tendencies. That's right! And that's why Bob and I planned our wedding for Wednesday, November 2, 1994.

In less than 16 years time, we've become directors of the 100 Marathon Club North America and the awesome Yakima River Canyon Marathon (YRCM) and are fondly known as the "world's oldest marathon race directors." Now in our eighties, we're both happy to have this title and grateful that Bob can still complete marathons.

Bob's first marathon was at age 51 at the Heart of America Marathon on Labor Day 1981 in Columbia, Missouri. His 100th marathon was at the same race 10 years later. His personal record of 3:00:12 was set in 1987 at the Emerald City Marathon in Seattle when he was 58. His total of 470 marathons (and counting) includes 44 ultramarathons, with the longest one being the completion of 101 miles in 23 hours at the Sri Chinmoy 24-Hour Race in Seattle.

Bob ranks number one in the Pacific Northwest, number 20 in the United States, and number 79 in the world for the number of completed marathons. His 400th marathon was run at our YRCM in 2007, and his goal is to run number 500 at this race on March 31, 2012. After that, he wants to become a 50-states finisher by completing the last 13 states that he needs.

Bob is frequently asked for training suggestions, so here is his list:

1. **Train for marathons by running marathons. I run one or two marathons every month and every weekend in the spring and fall for my 20 per year.**

2. **Run some of the same marathons every year and develop long strings. My longest one dates from 1985 to 2010 at the Capital City Marathon in Olympia, Washington.**

3. **Run some new marathons every year for the novelty.**

4. **Join a 50-states club to foster this goal.**

5. **Don't run injured. Try walking or run/walking while the injury is healing.**

6. **Run or walk marathons as long as you can. Thankfully, there is no age limit, just course-closing times that can be delayed by taking early starts.**

7. **Above all else, enjoy the marathoning sport and adventures. Be thankful if you are still running or walking marathons.**

I'm thankful that I was a Wednesday-night bride and grateful to be a part of this wonderful club as the nonrunning half of Team Dolphin.

Determined Not to Be Discouraged

by • Lena Christian

I am writing about my husband, Moses Christian, who is one of your Maniacs. Moses is a practicing physician and surgeon. He started running in 1993, and in 1994 he found out that he had prostate cancer. He was determined not to be discouraged and kept up his running.

For the last 15 years, he has run a marathon a month. He has not slowed down his activities. He also climbed Mount Kilimanjaro in 1996 and ran a marathon after he came down. He also bungee jumped in New Zealand in 2007. Four times he did the bike marathon along with the Los Angeles Marathon right afterward.

He does a lot of charity work in India in an orphanage and medical clinic and has gone other places around the world to help out. To date he has done 152 official marathons and 37 marathons of his own (and who is counting all the half-marathons?). At age 78, he still keeps up the monthly marathons, his practice, and his surgeries.

44

Dream Come True

by • Barb Wnek

In Anchorage recently, I finished my 86th marathon and have six states left to complete my 50-states quest. But my dream-come-true run wasn't a marathon and was only two blocks long. I was an Olympic torchbearer in 2004. I was chosen because of my creative teaching ideas. I teach physical education and health to kindergarten through sixth-grade students in St. Louis, Missouri. I use my book *Celebration Games: Physical Activities for Every Month*, which provides a calendar year's worth of physical fitness activities, skills, games, and rhythm and dance activities, each based on a specific holiday or seasonal theme. They're all designed to get 5- to 12-year-olds excited about physical activity. I received the Dole Five-a-Day Creative Teacher of the Year award. Olympian Jackie Joyner-Kersee spoke to my students. My marathon running motivates my students to live healthy, active lifestyles and to learn about all the places I run.

Maniac Friendship

by • Paige Kurtz and • Maria Poranski

Despite the extensive logistical challenges the race organizing committee faced because of Hurricane Katrina, the 2006 Mardi Gras Marathon went off as scheduled. I had to be there. The New Orleans Track Club put together a great run through the French Quarter, Midtown, the Garden District and back to the Superdome. It was a beautiful and very emotional event. After the marathon, I hung out on the terrace of the Superdome (which had not yet been reopened after the hurricane) for a while and chatted with several runners. I ate red beans, rice, and king cake and met a bunch of interesting people, including Maria and Charlie Surran. We ran into each other several times the next day while sightseeing and then ended up on the same flight out of New Orleans. We talked some more on the plane and exchanged e-mails before going our separate ways to Virginia and Florida.

We talked each other into meeting up in Delaware a few months later to run a marathon. Maria drove up from Virginia Beach, Virginia, where she lived, and I flew up from Melbourne, Florida, where I was living at the time. We all had a great time, and a friendship and running-traveling partnership had begun.

As fate would have it, my husband and I moved to the Virginia Beach area about four months after that. Maria and I started running together more and more and found that we both enjoyed traveling to different marathons. (Maria is a committed 50-stater. I am a member but more of just a marathon junkie who will go anywhere for a marathon.) We've been traveling to many marathons together over the past few years, seeking good local food and wineries, meeting new people, and having wacky fun. Often just the two of us make a trip, but occasionally we travel with others, and we've picked up a few new running chicks along the way. (My husband loves not having to go to all my marathons with me.)

We nicknamed ourselves the Running Chicks and ended up asking others to join us on our Facebook page. Here is our group description: *The Running Chicks celebrate the combination of many of the essentials of a happy life: fun with friends, marathon running, traveling, and drinking wine. We are 50-staters, Maniacs, speedsters, plodders, midpack, back-of-the-pack, six-pack, goal-oriented, dedicated, phfun-loving marathon hoes (and pimps?). This group is open to fellow runners, anyone we've met on our travels, and anyone who embraces the Running Chick lifestyle. (You don't have to be a chick!) The chick is our mascot, and she loves sharing adventures with us!*

At some point, Maria created "the running chick on a stick" so she could travel with us to marathons and wineries. Sometimes marshmallow Peeps make a trip, too—they're chicks!

We have shared many great marathon and travel experiences. We've danced for hours after the Chicago Marathon, cooled off in a public water fountain in St. Louis, scraped ice off the car on the way to the Myrtle Beach

Marathon, and flirted with the danger of frozen Gatorade spillage at the 2010 Mississippi Blues Marathon (max temp that day was about 32; what is it with these southern marathons?). We've observed a SWAT team on the roof of the Peabody in Little Rock, frolicked on the lawn of The Elms in Newport, Rhode Island, and helped rescue a passed-out bar patron after the Wineglass Marathon! We shared a fried Snickers bar after the Vegas Marathon (totally earned it!) and have gotten sidetracked driving out of the way to find local wineries near marathons around the United States. We particularly love sharing the antioxidant benefits of red wine from a local winery as a recovery beverage—even better with dark chocolate, of course!

We've also developed quirky marathon traditions, such as checking and loudly announcing the mile equivalents of the calorie content of bakery items in the grocery store. (One bottle of wine equals five miles of running; a pint of Ben and Jerry's ice cream equals approximately 13 miles—only a half-marathon!) We also make it a point to enjoy a bird's- (chick's-) eye view and a smattering of history in each city's tallest building and to explore various forms of public transportation. Pedicabs and boat tours are our favorites. I carry a duck call and quack at runners, spectators, and volunteers throughout my races (quacky running chick), and Maria frequently wears accessories on her visor (including cheese for Wisconsin, a tiny cowboy hat for Country Music, and a tiara on her birthday marathon). We both wear lipstick, because we are girlie chicks, but we are now aware of the need to be careful not to get run over by traffic while reapplying.

We made an attempt to craft our own wine at a local winery and named it Running Chicks Recovery Red—bin 26.2. Of course, we had the chick on the label.

I persuaded Maria to wait to join Marathon Maniacs because I told her it was soft to join at just one star, even though she had earned it some time ago (she felt totally inadequate and readily agreed!). I could join at two stars, but that seemed a bit weak as well. So of course, we talked ourselves into doing a double in New Hampshire and Maine in October 2009 so we could join with four stars. We tried to coordinate our applications so that we would have sequential numbers, but apparently it was a busy week for MM apps, so we're #1831 and #1834. We've now completed over 20 marathons in 20 states together, with many more planned. As Maria says: "I'll tour the world 26 miles, 385 yards at a time."

46

It's All About the Food

by • Perky Garcia

Why am I a Marathon Maniac? It is all about the food. Trail marathons have everything: 26.2ish miles of beautiful scenery, great people, and a bunch of all-you-can-eat buffet tables along the course. It just doesn't get any better!

The marks of a good marathon are sore abs from laughing, a sore throat from yelling, and sore arms from waving. *Perfect*!

125

One of Those Marathon Things Looks Interesting

by • Pam Medhurst

I started running in 1977. I just decided one day to go out and run. I had on a pair of Levi's and some regular tennis shoes. I ran three blocks, came home, and my husband of one year laughed and said, "That's it?"

I stuck it out and added a few blocks at a time until I could do three whole miles. Never one to do things the easy way, I thought that doing one of those marathon things looked interesting. My husband said I could never do something like that. I guess that after only a year, he didn't know me all that well, plus running starts giving a person some strong inner thoughts, so I kept at it and I did indeed finish my first marathon. It was the Heart of San Diego and finished in a stadium. I still have the shirt, although it's pretty threadbare now.

I've completed close to 200 marathons since then, including the Tahoe Triple, the Goofy Challenge, Catalina, Big Sur, and a few ultras. I'm still married to the same guy, but he never says that I can't do something—he's afraid of what I'll turn that into!

Running really does give you the confidence to go for it, no matter what "it" is. There have been some real moments out there—finishing the race and not finding a way back to the hotel (before cell phones) and wandering

around strange locations praying for a taxi or a pay phone. It was so cold while running the Los Angeles Marathon in the pouring rain that when I stopped to pee at a gas station, my hands were too cold to pull my tights back up. People were pounding on the door. I couldn't decide whether I should waddle to the door and ask a fellow runner to pull my pants up. In the end, I ran my hands under the hot water long enough to get my fingers to work. I also remember having heat problems at Lake Tahoe but reviving enough to continue the race.

I remember reading an article once that wondered how many marathons you had to run before you either gave some of the shirts away or cut the sleeves off so you had a tank. At the time, every shirt was so special that I couldn't imagine cutting one. The day I finally created a sleeveless version of one of the marathon shirts, I knew that I had reached a whole new level.

Yup, I'm a runner!

48

Meeting the Maniacs

by • Pamela Brulotte

I remember the day that I met the Main Maniacs as though it was yesterday. I was sitting in the Richland, Washington, Shilo Inn breakfast area trying to will my stomach to slurp down some instant oatmeal on the morning of October 26, 2003, before the marathon. I was 31, a wife, restaurant owner, and mother of three, and I had just run the Portland Marathon with two fellow marathon mamas.

During breakfast, I overheard Tony Phillippi, Chris Warren, and Steve Yee talking about "Marathon Maniacs." I joined in to say that I had just run a marathon and was about to do another. They talked about whether I qualified as a Maniac with those two marathons. I wasn't feeling much like a Maniac, just a hard worker who liked to eat a lot (sausage and beer) and thus liked to run to stay in shape. It was never really determined whether I qualified as a Maniac, but I was trying to get psyched up about running yet another 26.2 miles. It still seemed like an overwhelming number of miles to run since I had never participated in sports in high school and had struggled with asthma for most of my life.

The gun went off, and I soon found myself running with Steve, Chris, and Jen Yogi. I don't quite remember what we talked about since I was just trying to keep up with them for as long as I could and get as many tips as possible from these amazing runners. Before I knew it, we were at mile 13 and were keeping up a great pace.

They then started to feed these crazy thoughts to me that I was on pace to qualify for the Boston Marathon (I needed a 3:40). They were so positive and confident in me that I just kept plugging along. I was still questioning whether I could do it when I found myself alone at mile 20 after Chris and Jen had started to pull ahead and Steve slowed down a bit to wrestle with stomach problems. The clock said 2:35, and I knew that I had a chance to qualify but would have to keep up my pace and not slow down. The miles seemed to take forever to pass until I found myself within sight of the finish line, where my family was standing. I dug deep and crossed the finish line in 3:31 (coincidentally, my bib number that day!). I was ecstatic and could not stop smiling. I had done something that I had never thought was possible.

Since that day, I have finished 18 marathons (I officially became a Maniac in 2006) and several triathlons and the Ironman Coeur D'Alene. I ran into Tony there and was encouraged each time I saw him ahead of me on the course.

Every event I participate in seems to have Maniacs throughout. Every time I see one, I get an extra burst of encouragement through our shared camaraderie!

The Timeout Chair

by • Paul Gentry

As a Marathon Maniac, I find that race memories tend to drift off into a healthy blur. How can a true Maniac remember crossing all those finish lines? Instead, you look obsessively forward, planning the multiple roads ahead. You can't help yourself; it's a genetic defect, part of the character makeup that defines this insane running club. With that said, I can only remember that the following happened in 2008 at one of my eight marathons that year.

We have all learned that good hydration is a must, but there is a certain side effect that you can't control. If nature calls, you go with the flow! Porta-potties are not always in abundance, and there is an unwritten marathon code that if you notice someone off to the side of the road near trees or shrubbery, you quickly look away and focus your eyes straight ahead.

I remember plodding along at an 11-minute pace, knowing that a PR was out of the question, with my eyes turning yellow. I would have even considered finding relief on a residential front lawn, but fortunately I spotted a very welcome sight ahead of me. Lined up side by side were two porta-potties with only three runners waiting! Little did I know that I would soon witness an off-the-wall occurrence that would never fade into that blur of Maniac memories.

An extra two minutes was no longer an issue, so I took my spot in line behind two guys and a lady. Suddenly, from out of nowhere, a stealthy marathon runner swooped in like an eagle shooting straight into the then-opening porta-potty door. Before he closed the door, he glanced directly at us, smiled like the Grinch, and said, "You snooze, you lose; I'm in a hurry!"

My mind was racing a mile a minute while I stood idle. Surely proper marathon etiquette had just been violated as we silently watched in shock as the green vacancy color turned to a rude red! Did this just happen? Did that scrawny, middle-aged marathoner figuratively slap us all in the face? It was like walking into a Hell's Angels biker bar, breaking a pool stick over someone's skull, and then stepping back and blurting out, "Now what are you going to do about it?" We were stunned at the audacity!

Tick, tock went the clock for all of us; no Boston qualifier today. Before I could think of something appropriate to say to the offender, I heard the irritated voice of one of the other poor saps in line. "Dude, we can't just let this happen." As luck would have it, the two men whose place in line had been usurped were Clydesdale runners, those who have a remarkable combination of girth and endurance! I muttered a quick "Thank you, God!" knowing that justice would soon be served!

The Goliath runner said to his brother in arms, "Count off two minutes." Then, like a man possessed, he proceeded to wrap his arms around the porta-potty door as the runner, right on cue, attempted to exit.

His muffled voice yelled, "Hey, let me out of here, I'm losing time!"

"Sorry, two-minute penalty," was the reply, which was so appropriate that it made us all burst into laughter.

By now I had noticed that the other porta-potty was available, but I didn't care and continued watching while the two-minute countdown was verbally concluded.

When the frazzled runner finally made his exit, he looked at us like a boy facing bullies in the schoolyard, said, "Guess I had that coming," and trotted away. He knew that he had been a bad boy who deserved this punishment! The marathon code was honorably upheld, and we high-fived each other and continued on with our marathons. I haven't run into this boorish lout since, but when I do, I hope he is standing dutifully in a long line!

Disclaimer: No Marathon Maniacs were involved in this crime against humanity! 🐱

50

Race Nails

by • Linda Garbo

There are some not-so-serious parts to running that add to the fun. On the serious side, we do our training, watch our diets, work with our mental strategies, plan the race details and logistics, and get psyched up before we go. Some of us have stepped out of the box a bit and put a little last-minute sass into making the event special, especially the marathon.

A few years ago, my friend and I got into the New York City Marathon through the lottery. We were thrilled and decided to do it up right. As we were running those long training runs, we began talking about getting our nails done to celebrate the marathon. We decided to get them done with a patriotic theme. We drew up our design, each nail done differently but with a common red, white, and blue motif. We placed different decals on our nails to spice them up. We brought our mocked-up drawing to our nail artist and *voilà,* we flew to New York City to run with what we know were the best-looking nails there! They were the start of a tradition for marathon-distance races or beyond.

Since then, we've designed and run with some of the most outrageous nails ever. My nail artist loves it when I'm marathon bound because she gets to be as creative as she can. We try to have them customized to the theme of the race. Rock 'n' Roll marathons with music themes, Avenue of the Giants with naturelike, hippie influence, and when we were both running as new Maniacs, we even ran with Marathon Maniac nails for the Chicago Marathon.

Run, and rock on!

Marathon Courses
as Passion and Art

by • Rodney Chang

I made it into the Marathon Maniacs at age 64, making me one of the oldest members. Now running like a snail (I used to run under four hours in my 30s), why did I bother joining when many other members still care about beating their current personal-best finishing time? For me, crossing yet another finish line is self-fulfilling.

But what keeps me competing is art! As I search online to schedule runs, I find inadequate visualization of marathon courses and no data at all about crowd support or the quality of the scenery. So I came up with the idea of carrying several cameras to document whole 26-mile routes, including every mile-marker reference. Suddenly, I had a personal motivation, a mission, to keep me going.

I now participate in full marathons, not for time but in search of the best scene along a specific course that I, as an artist, can turn into a beautiful framed landscape. At the same time, I feel that I am contributing to our marathon sport by providing a review of courses at my site for those searching for scenic marathon experiences as well as to get some idea of crowd support (see *www.marathoncoursephotos.com*). This cause isn't cheap, as I have to fly back and forth from Hawaii to the Mainland races. It costs about $1,500 to

$2,000 for each marathon weekend trip. I still work full time, so this cost doesn't include lost revenue from taking time off from my small business.

This year, I need five more full marathons to get that coveted fourth-star status as a Maniac (nine marathons in 12 months). My knees chronically hurt. I hope I make it.

52

A Marathoning Hobby

by • Tom Hosner

Marathoners are by nature collectors of finisher's medals, running shirts, bibs, posters, and other items associated with running. My license-plate hobby now includes a collection of vanity license plates with running-related content, marathon signs, and other marathon memorabilia. As a member of Automobile License Plate Collectors Association (ALPCA), I have the opportunity to purchase custom novelty plates at the annual national convention and regional ALPCA meets as a way to raise funds for the club. The funds are primarily used to support the publishing of the club newsletter, the club website, and the convention/meeting expenses. As an example, the inaugural Hard Corps Marathon was held on April 25, 2009, at Camp Pendleton in Southern California.

On the same day, our local ALPCA Socal Region held a license-plate meet in the Marine Corps Mechanized Museum at Camp Pendleton. I had ordered two custom license plates for the meet with "26MILE" and "118" to coincide with the completion of my 118th marathon. I ran the marathon in the morning and drove over to the meet for lunch and picked up the license plates. The marathon finisher's medal with the Marine Corps logo looks great with the custom license plates.

I signed up for the 2010 Boston 2 Big Sur Challenge after qualifying for Boston at the 2009 San Francisco Marathon. I ordered the two motorcycle license plates shown in the photo on page 136 from the ALPCA Gold Rush Region in Northern California. Photos of the custom license plates were published in the Big Sur Marathon program. I am planning on completing the 2012 Boston 2 Big Sur.

In 2007, to celebrate my 100th marathon, I had a street sign made that read:

The street sign went to the Rock 'n' Roll Marathon in San Diego along with my two daughters, who were running their first marathon. After the marathon, I took the sign from my gear bag and had my daughters and six friends sign it and write comments on the back. It is a special souvenir for the milestone marathon. The "RUN 100" license plate that I bought on eBay is displayed among the other marathon memorabilia in my garage.

Next up on my running agenda was to finish a 100-mile run. A street sign hangs in my garage as a constant reminder of this running goal. In August 2010, my wife and I went to the Lean Horse 100 in Hot Springs, South Dakota, and I finished my first 100-miler.

I continue to collect marathon and ultra finishes along with a few special souvenir signs and license plates to enjoy my marathoning hobby.

My Favorite
Running Story

by • Steve Wisner

My 22-year-old daughter, Shannon, was with me when we visited a booth where Dick Beardsley was signing his book during the April 2008 Boston Marathon expo. I purchased one of his books and told him about my marathon schedule for the remainder of the year, which included the Athens Marathon in November.

I had won the trip through the Athens exchange program as part of the Houston Marathon earlier that year. This included a three-day cruise around the Greek islands and concluded with the classic marathon from the town of Marathon into Athens on November 9. During the conversation, Dick said to Shannon, "Why don't you make a deal with your dad that if you run the marathon, you get to go with him to Greece?" I responded that this would be impossible because Shannon had never run in any race and doesn't like running.

This really got Shannon going. She exclaimed, "I'm going with you, and I'm running the marathon."

Of course, the rest is history. Shannon proceeded to run her first race on August 7 (the Moonlight Margarita run in Austin), followed by the Nike

Human Race in Austin, and then she trained really hard and ran a half-marathon in Houston on October 26 (in a time of 2:20:47).

We both went to Greece and had the time of our lives visiting the Greek islands of Santorini, Mykonos, and Rhodes, along with a trip to Ephesus in Turkey. The trip concluded with both of us finishing the Athens Marathon (Dad in 3:43:42 and Shannon in 5:38:30).

We have Dick Beardsley to thank for some great father-daughter memories that will last a lifetime.

Shannon is currently teaching English in Prague, Czech Republic.

I ran into Dick Beardsley at the Royal Victoria Marathon in British Columbia last year and told him the story. He remembered us since he had also signed our bibs in Boston.

Father and Son

by • Stephen Bucken

My collegiate soccer dreams became financially impossible when I heard that my soccer scholarships had not come through. I asked my dad if he wanted to take a run to blow off some steam.

It was Thanksgiving morning. My dad and I embarked on our first run at a more-than-leisurely pace. Soccer had always been the connecting point for my dad and me, and although we didn't know it yet, this first eight-mile run would change our relationship forever.

As we ran, I remember joking with him, "Come on, Pops, what do you say we run a marathon?" Both of us could only laugh at the overwhelming thought of running 26.2 miles. But with my overcompetitive nature, I raced home and found that our hometown Sarasota Marathon was coming up in a little under three months. Being gluttons for punishment, my dad and I were back out on the road three short days later, slowly adding to our mileage. By Christmas, the goals were set: I was to run the Sarasota Marathon, and my dad would run the half-marathon.

Two months of crammed training later, we both had finished our races, and the addiction to distance running had set in. With the desire to race again, my dad and I began our search for our next race, but this time Dad wanted to go the full 26.2-mile distance.

Our race came in the 2010 Walt Disney World Marathon. The next 10 months of training took us through a lot but also kept us close and connected. I left for my first semester of college at the University of Florida in June, something not easy for any parent. But we made sure not to let the distance separate us; we talked all the time, with running often being the central topic of conversation. So although we could no longer take the runs together, we still both knew that the other would be waiting to hear split times and averages later that night. This motivation carried me all the way until I arrived home for Thanksgiving break of my fall semester. And on that Thanksgiving morning, exactly one year after our first run together, we set out on a 20-mile run, the last test to make sure my dad was ready for Disney. The run went off without a hitch, and we finished in awe of how far we had come together in the past year, not just as runners but also as father and son.

I went back to college for finals but returned soon thereafter for Christmas break, and my father and I began to taper and make final preparations for our big race. Race day came faster than either of us had expected, and now all the hype and anxiety would finally come to an end. On an ice-cold morning in Orlando, on January 10, 2010, my father and I set out to complete our journey.

We ran through the Walt Disney World parks and laughed about the days when he had dragged me through those parks as a kid. Now it was my turn to drag him through those same parks to the finish line. I remember the tears welling up in my eyes as we entered Epcot with only a mile to go, realizing that we were in fact going to cross the line together. And then our moment came, our moment to cross that finish line hand in hand as father and son, as marathoners.

We rounded the final corner, and as we heard the crowd roar, I could no longer hold back the emotion, and neither could my dad. I grabbed my father's hand and hoisted it in the air. We had done it; we had completed the marathon. We had remained best friends, and in that moment we embodied everything that truly is a father-and-son story.

Written for Klaus Bucken: my hero, my friend, my dad.

The Running Preacher

by • Dave Johnson

I mentioned to a friend at college that I had a goal to run a marathon one day. He, a track star, gave me a training schedule. I kept that marathon-training paper for the next 26 years and decided at the age of 46 that I had better run it sooner than later. A close friend gave me further encouragement. He told me that since I was the pastor of a small church trying to pay off its debt, he would donate $10 for every mile I ran and would double it if I finished the marathon. We announced it to the church, challenged the members to get involved, and soon even the young children were donating a penny a mile to pay off our debt.

The Fort Worth Cowtown Marathon was a perfect fit on my running calendar, so I registered. Through the years, I had run one-and-a-half to four miles on a regular basis, so I was excited by each new long run. The 10-mile barrier was tough until a church member's son visited one Sunday and informed me that I needed to drink liquid to go beyond this distance. As silly as that sounds now, in early 2000 I didn't know any marathon runners or how to use the Internet for research.

The thrill of running my first marathon at Cowtown that day gave way to panic, fear, and, finally, to a grim determination to see it through. I made the rookie mistake of going out too fast and at mile two a "charley horse" grabbed my right hamstring. I struggled for the next six miles, walking a lot, and finished the first half at a miserable pace. As bad as the first half went, the second half was pure joy, and I even cried at the finish. A great memory from every race is the conversation with other runners, sharing our stories and encouraging one another. I felt strong with two miles to go, so I told the fellow I was running with at the time that I would see him at the finish. I can still hear him hollering after me as I took off, "Run, preacher, run!" It turned out to be a prophetic statement.

The run raised a lot of money but did not completely pay off the debt, so I found another marathon three months later in Amarillo. To help promote this one, I confidently said that I would shave my head if I did not beat my previous time. What I learned was that each race is its own adventure based on my body, the terrain, the temperature, and other elements. My family was concerned as the clock ticked, but I pushed through and beat my first time by all of two minutes. The next month, due to the great generosity of our church, the debt was paid off, and I was hooked on marathons.

Three months later, I ran the Roswell, New Mexico, Turtle Marathon and enjoyed it, but I found that I missed having a cause to run for. Five months later, I was in Austin and ran for an injured high school football player. The Sunday we presented his check from our supportive church and community, I was asked to run for a sick baby girl. So two months later, I did the Oklahoma City Memorial Marathon. When we gave the check to the family, someone asked me to run for a lady dying of cancer. A month later, I was back in Amarillo and ran for her. The *Odessa American* newspaper did some stories on these events, and the writer labeled me the "running preacher."

Over the next seven years as a pastor, I continued to run for people, causes, and organizations. My community honored me with the Heritage Award for Religion, largely based on my running and the big donating hearts of my church, community, family, and friends. I retired as pastor in May 2007 but have continued my running, and I am currently establishing a nonprofit organization, Running Preacher Ministries, "to inspire fitness for all ages to help somebody." Not everybody wants to run marathons and ultras, but all people should find what they love to do, stay active, and help others.

I've always enjoyed a mixture of marathons and ultrarunning, especially trail running. Currently, I'm within reach of completing 52 marathons or ultra runs in 52 weeks. You can check my Marathon Maniac #1440 page (on the Maniacs website) and see if my goal has been accomplished. Lord willing, I would like to keep running, seeing old friends, meeting new ones, and adding to the approximately $500,000 raised for the needs of others until He puts me at the starting line on the heavenly trails and streets of gold.

Sleeping With My Wife

by • Cheri Damitio

I was running in the inaugural Seattle Rock 'n' Roll marathon in June 2009. It was early in the marathon, and it was crowded. I heard some raucous shouting coming from behind me, followed by a man's voice yelling, "Hey! Weren't you the one who was sleeping with my wife?" I was eager for a bit of distraction, so like a lot of other folks, I turned around to see who was shouting and which poor fellow was being confronted. Even at some distance, I could see right away that the person causing the commotion was wearing a Marathon Maniac singlet. I didn't recognize him but thought to myself, *What a weirdo; how embarrassing for the club*.

Then the guy picked up his pace and yelled again louder as he weaved through the sea of runners in pursuit of someone, "Hey! Aren't *you* the one who was sleeping with my wife?" I looked back at him again because he was getting closer. *Oh, great,* I thought, *Now he's got his camera phone pointed over this way to take a picture! I've got to get out of here because I don't want to be in that photo*. I tried to speed up and wondered again who the poor guy was who was getting called out. He must be nearby. Then the Maniac ran up next to me and introduced himself as Betsy's husband, Matt. The light went on. "Oh, yeah, I guess I did sleep with your wife," I replied sheepishly.

I met Maniac Betsy Rogers at the Yakima River Canyon Marathon in April 2009 and shared a room (and bed!) to save expenses.

57

Going the Distance

by • Letty Marino

Many people gasp incredulously when they find that I have run several marathons. Some of their comments are: "Why would anyone want to run that far?" "If I want to go that far, I just get in my car," or simply, "Are you insane?"

In today's society, everyone seems to be looking for a spiritual or life-altering experience. I believe that I have found that experience through training for and running a marathon. I've learned that I control my own life, that I am never alone, and that it's not just OK but important to feel proud of myself.

The decision to run a marathon did not happen suddenly but came over a period of time. Going through a difficult time in my life, it seemed as though no matter what I did, nothing ever went my way. I suddenly found myself as a single working mother of two very active boys. The only thing that kept me sane was my daily three-mile run. This was my time alone with my thoughts and emotions, time to sort out what was real and what I had fabricated. Yes, he was cheating, and no, he didn't love me.

It was a time also to put in perspective the current crisis I was facing. Did I really need to fix the air conditioner, or could we get through June so I could afford to give my son a birthday party?

When angry or frustrated, I ran hard and fast until I was too exhausted to feel anything. Depressed, I ran slowly, gradually picking up the pace as my mood was lifted by the rhythmic sounds of my stride and the comforting aches of sore muscles. This was real, something I could control. You want to pass me? Go ahead, I've set my pace, and no one is going to pressure me to go any faster. Someone's in my way—not a problem; I'll just go around. Nothing is holding me back!

Soon I became a regular on the running course, recognizing other runners. I belonged! It didn't matter what I wore, how fast, how slowly, or how far I ran or that my life was in shambles. I was a runner, a member of a special group of people. Quickly picking up the lingo, I found that PB had nothing to do with peanut butter sandwich, fartlek was nothing to be embarrassed about, and carboloading did not involve a truck—all vital things to keep in mind when talking to seasoned runners.

Three miles was no longer enough. It was four and then five—but that's all, since I had only an hour to run, shower, and get back to work. Then someone mentioned the Marine Corps Marathon—only 26.2 miles. It was now the end of June. Could I be ready by October?

Five members of my running family quickly rallied around me. We would all run the race together. I had the fever, but finding the time to train would be tricky. A neighbor offered to see the boys off to school three times a week so I could get in a six-mile run before work because soccer practice, dinner, and homework took up the evenings. On Saturdays, I could do a long run before the boys woke up if I was out the door by 6:00 A.M. and back in time for a shower and then off to soccer games. Adding one mile each weekend, by mid-October, I was up at 5:00 A.M., putting in a 20-mile run, and back before wakeup. Thankfully, soccer season had ended in early September so the rest of the day could be spent nursing my sore muscles and watching rental videos or playing board games. Oh, there were many times that I wanted to give up. It would have been much easier to sleep in and not feel so tired during the week, but what kept me going was that I had come so far, and the thought of giving up seemed to encompass more than just failing to run a marathon. I could do this, and I had to do this; at the time, I didn't know why.

Finally, the day of the big event arrived. The boys were dropped off at their dad's for the weekend, and they wished me luck. A friend offered to drive me to the race and back; I had a stick shift and didn't know whether my legs could make the drive home. Due to injuries or other commitments, of the original six runners, I was the only one running the marathon. Thoughts of fear and failure crammed my brain but quickly gave way to excitement as we lined up in the start corrals. I looked down at the timing chip laced in my shoe and said a quick prayer that I would still be standing when I crossed the finish line.

The gun went off, and a cheer went through the crowd. The first six miles were run on pure adrenaline. At mile seven, I realized that I had started too fast and that if I didn't slow down, I would be hitting The Wall too soon. It was hard, but I slowed down to a 10-minute-mile pace, enjoying the spectators cheering us on. Locals crowded the streets offering water, Power Bars, Vaseline, or any other tidbit that might help a faltering runner. They motivate runners by calling their names if they are written on their shirts, and if not, spectators still yell out something like "Way to go, gal in the green shorts! You're my hero!" This ego boost is enough to last a mile. Even children line the streets, reaching out their hands in hopes that a runner will give them five as they run past. I soaked all this up, realizing that I had earned this experience, that it was reserved only for those running the race.

Mile 13: Halfway there—and even though it is only 47 degrees and raining, I am not cold as long as I keep moving.

I think about how far I've come in my life. I have a good job; I bought a car and house on my own. The boys and I endured a lot of hardships but are much better off now. Thank you, God.

Mile 18: We're entering "Hell's Point," so nicknamed by runners because it is a three-mile peninsula with no cheering spectators to keep you going. This is where most people hit The Wall. It is eerily quiet except for the steady swish-swoosh of soaked feet hitting the pavement.

Mile 19: People dropping out, saying what I'm afraid to think: "I can't go anymore." "It's not worth it." "It hurts too much." I can't listen to the negative thoughts. I have to get away from them. I pick up the pace, but somehow others follow me.

You can't make it on your own with two boys.
Why don't you just come home and live with Mom and Dad?
Give me the boys. I can support them better than you can.

I run harder and get the hell out of Hell's Point. At mile 24, my right calf hurts so much that I have to stop and stretch. A stranger rushes up and starts massaging my muscle, which has a noticeable spasm. "Don't give up," he says, "You're almost home." Thank you for the angel, God.

Mile 25 point something: It's all uphill from here—literally. The last part of the marathon is up the hill heading toward the Iwo Jima Memorial. What lunatic thought this one up?

Suddenly, everything falls into perspective.

The words of John "The Penguin" Bingham run through my mind: *The miracle isn't that I finished. The miracle is that I had the courage to start.* Tears of joy sting my eyes as I cross the finish line. My legs are like lead, and I am very close to hypothermia, but all I can think about is that hunk of metal strung on a ribbon around my neck. I did it! I went the distance and survived!

Running With Wendy

by • Danny Lyon

Goal—under four hours.

Announcements, start gun, and in no time, at 10K saying "Hi" to my wife, Connie, and kids.

Feeling good at 16K.

Out of nowhere, goose bumps, a stitch in my side, and my pace drops. Dehydration? I can't believe it.

Runners stream by while I mutter to myself, blaming, complaining.

At 20K, the course leaves the main road for narrow pathways along the Bow River. The only sounds are my footsteps. I'm feeling sorry for myself. A female runner shuffles by wearing signs saying "Blind runner." Instead of being amazed, my "Oh, woe is me" self whispers, "Even blind runners are passing you."

At the next aid station, volunteers are concerned about her running alongside the river. Forgetting that I'm miserable, I blurt out, "I'll go with her," and clarify, "If I can catch her."

Funny what a change of focus does. I convert anxiousness to catch her before she falls in the river into the best form and pace I had all day. When I catch her, the real marathon begins.

I'm running with Wendy, a marvel, a no-fear person.

By herself, how? In sunshine, shadows off edges or curbs could act as a guide.

Blind since? Birth.

Training? Indoor track; inside rail as her guide; longest 20 miles.

Why a marathon? A running milestone and longtime goal.

Other sports? School swim team. Smiling, she says, "You hit the lane dividers a lot."

Track, daily before school started—wasn't allowed to compete.

Now at college, cross-country team—finally competed in a race (with a guide). "Scratchy through the trees," Wendy says, smiling.

Family support? Her aunt waiting at the finish line.

Thirty kilometers, sun beating down, the pace slows, and we might finish after the course closes. I ask volunteers to radio a request to keep the finish line assembled with a race photographer on hand for Wendy's official photo.

One step past 32K (20 miles), arms in the air, shouting, we had a big celebration. Every step is now a personal distance record for her. For the first time I hear, "My legs are stiff; how much farther?"

Despite what now had to be pain with each step, she never complains—it wasn't her style. Instead, celebrations at each kilometer marker continue.

Connie meets us at kilometer 40, relaying Wendy's accomplishment to Connie's sister, our three kids, and two nieces waiting at the finish.

Exiting the trees that shade the last 2K, all five kids run for us. "Are you really blind?" "Can you see me when I jump in front of you?" "Can you see me to the side like this?" "Can you watch TV?" "Do you have homework?" "Do you go to school?" "Can you drive?" I ask them to mind their manners. Wendy insists that it's OK, that kids are the best to talk with about her blindness.

Finish line intact, a photographer indeed on hand, only a few are left to witness what is, in my opinion, one of the most outstanding marathon finishes ever.

Fifteen meters left, I tell her that she should be finishing on her own; to run, not walk across; and to extend her arms in the air when she felt the timing mats. A perfect finish, a medal, and an emotional hug from an ecstatic aunt.

Excellent stuff.

My son announced that he could tell everyone that his dad finished dead last in the Calgary Marathon. Dead last, yes, but it was the best finish I have ever had.

When someone tells me he or she can't or I question my abilities, I think back to Wendy's inspiration and determination.

"Go to the edge, jump off, and develop wings on the way down."—Ray Bradbury.

As far as I could tell, Wendy had done exactly that for all of her young life.

59

Taking Control

by • Brandon Mead

The answer to why I run is not as simple as to get in shape; rather, a series of events led me to where I am today as a runner.

My journey started because I was a quitter, starting in elementary school. Whenever practice got hard, I would stop or ask for a break. It eventually led to my quitting football in my senior year in high school two weeks before the end of the season because I didn't want to practice in the rain. The excuse I told my coach was that I wasn't getting enough playing time, which was true. I didn't play a lot, not because the coach didn't like me, but because I quit when practice became hard.

This quitting attitude stayed with me into the Army. Somehow I made it through basic training without quitting, and I thought that I had finally changed and put my quitting days behind me. I was wrong. After basic training I went to airborne school, where I failed my physical fitness test. When offered the option to stay two weeks to get in shape and continue with my training, I quit. I blamed the sergeants, saying they were purposely failing soldiers to clear up space.

This was not true. I was just out of shape.

My quitting started to evolve into a blame game. Whenever I failed or quit the Army Physical Fitness Test (APFT), I blamed my leaders for not training me right. Every time I failed a height and weight test, I would blame the chow hall for not having good, healthy food, not my obsession with fast food and candy. I was blaming the stress of the Army for my alcohol, tobacco, and drug use. I had the attitude that I could control nothing in my life.

On July 20, 2007, my attitude began to change. This was our platoon's first taste of real combat in Iraq. We were struck by a large improvised explosive device (IED) under my driver's seat and were unable to locate the triggerman (who set off the IED). When we finally arrived back at the base 12 hours later, our Stryker combat vehicle broke down, and I passed out from a combination of a concussion and exhaustion. I was given three days of light duty after this incident.

Less than a week later, another vehicle in our platoon was struck by a large IED. Shrapnel went through the vehicle and severed three fingers on the driver's hand. The Stryker was destroyed. We continued the mission and found multiple IEDs on August 1, 2007. I was driving a Stryker when the IED hit, and the vehicle was launched many feet in the air. Our lieutenant shattered his jaw and was sent home. Two other soldiers were medevaced, and I along with two other soldiers suffered concussions. Our Stryker was destroyed. The unit sent out to recover our squad's vehicle was struck by another large IED. The soldiers were transported by vehicle back to the base. One of these soldiers was sent to Germany, which means serious injuries were suffered. I never heard anything after that. Our vehicle was recovered many hours later.

Two weeks later, the 1st squad was struck by a large IED, and two of the soldiers were medevaced. One soldier was sent home due to a major traumatic brain injury. He never came back to the unit. The 1st squad's Stryker was also destroyed. The company deployed with 10 Stryker vehicles, all of which were destroyed in Iraq. Many other vehicles we used we were destroyed as well.

The one thing we could not figure out is how no one in our company died. Our mission as combat engineers was to look for IEDs, and we found many. We were also blown up multiple times. Some in the unit were struck 10 or more times. Other units we deployed were struck far less than us and lost multiple soldiers. There were quite a few missions where we missed an IED and soldiers coming behind us were killed. Sometimes our mission would have us turn around at certain points that we would find out later were just short of an IED that killed multiple soldiers. It would always bother us—sometimes piss us off—when we would hear of a soldier dying by an IED blast. It was our job to find them, and we found many and I am sure we saved many lives. Often we would get hit and never see who pulled the trigger. It was frustrating. I sometimes think of the IEDs missed on my long runs, and when I wanted to quit, I would remember that there are people who could no longer do what I am doing, and this pushes me to keep going.

I started thinking about the things that I could and could not control. This is when I started regaining control of my life. I began eating healthier and working out. I also began to stop thinking about drugs and alcohol because I hated the feeling of not being in control.

I started working out constantly, not just because I wanted to be in better shape but also because I didn't want people to think that I was a quitter. I went from being a failure on the APFT to being the most in-shape person in the company and maxing my test. This is also when I began running. When I returned home in the summer of 2008, I ran my first half-marathon and then a full marathon. I recently completed my first two 50Ks in 15 days to join the Maniacs and look forward to running farther in the future. I now run to prove to people that I am no longer a quitter and to find my physical and mental limits.

Through this experience, I have learned that far too often we try to blame other people or outside forces for our own failures and shortcomings, and the first step to overcoming this is recognizing what you can control in your life and taking that control back.

When I Grow Up, Can I Be Bob?

by • Ed "Mad Hatter-Fancy Pants" Ettinghausen

I met Bob Dolphin for the first time at about mile eight of the Boston Marathon in 2010. I was going quite a bit slower than my 3:29 BQ because I was nursing a tibia stress fracture, so I did the whole Boston course in a big black support boot. But this story is really about Bob. After I finished the marathon, I went back out to meet Bob and a runner who goes by the name "Maine-iac"and came in with them. Bob was bloodied up from a bad cut that he had suffered in a fall at mile 19, but he was bound and determined to finish the race. He came in, got his Boston finisher's medal, went straight to the medical tent, and then had an ambulance ride to the hospital—eight stitches!

I went to the Marathon Maniacs dinner that evening at Johns Hopkins Pub and proceeded to tell all the Maniacs how Bob had cut his head in a fall but had toughed it out to the end. Two days later, I learned that Bob had actually cut his hand, not his head, but with all the bystanders cheering, it sounded to me like Maine-iac had said his head. Besides, Bob had a bloody cap and a bloody cloth in his hand.

I later learned that the local news crew had gotten video footage of all three of us coming in like the Three Musketeers, or more appropriately, like three soldiers in the Revolutionary War (it was Patriots' Day, after all). All three of us wore our matching yellow MM jerseys— Maine-iac on the left looking battle weary, Bob in the middle with bloody head and hands, and me on the right with my big black boot! A friend said she saw the footage replayed on the local news the next morning.

Six days later, back on the West Coast at the Big Sur Marathon, I saw Bob again. We played leapfrog on the hills. Bob passed me on the downhills with his stitched-up hand not even wrapped up, and I passed Bob on the uphills, still in my big old support boot. Well, Big Sur is known for its rugged coastal beauty as well as the rugged coastal hills, which seem predominantly up!

I finished the marathon just within the six-hour cutoff but didn't see Bob. I went back out and found him at around mile 25. He was struggling a bit but was getting it done! What's that motto? Once a Marine, always a Marine!

So Marine Bob and I come in, he's dead friggin' last, and his wife, Lenore, and his daughter are waiting for him at what used to be the finish line. A cute young college girl comes up to Bob, gives him a flower, and plants a big wet kiss on him! Lenore doesn't even bat an eye. They were out of finisher's medals (actually, the medals are ceramic), so the woman who holds the female course record—Svetlana Vasilyeva—gives Bob her finisher's medal and says, "You deserve this more than me. I'll get another one!" When I grow up, can I be Bob?

Postscript: *Ed was eventually able to break free from the boot and got back to running again (after one false start that required an additional two months in the boot). He has now completed 150 marathons and ultras, including 12 of 100 miles or longer. He won the Runner's World/New Balance Movement Challenge in 2010 for most race miles in a year—over 3,000. On July 11-12, he competed in the 2011 Badwater 135 Ultramarathon, referred to as "the toughest footrace on the planet." That race completed his Guinness World Record for the most marathons in 365 days by a man. Badwater was his 135th marathon or ultramarathon in 365 days as well as his 200th lifetime marathon or ultramarathon. All but 10 of those have been as a Marathon Maniac.*

Challenge Yourself

by • Yolanda Holder, aka Walking Diva

I joined the Marathon Maniacs in September 2007. I didn't know that becoming a Maniac would change my life.

Before becoming a Maniac, I had done only two or three marathons and a few half-marathons a year. In 2008, I was turning 50 years young and wanted to do something different for my 50th birthday. I decided to walk 50 marathons in 50 weeks.

I accomplished more than this goal. I walked 65 marathons or ultras and became Marathon Maniac of the year for 2008. In 2009, I wasn't sure what I wanted to do, but I still had that exciting and wonderful high that I get after finishing a marathon. I did 77 marathons or ultras and became Marathon Maniac of the year for 2009.

On this amazing journey, I have learned much about myself.

I have stepped out of my comfort zone. I have pushed my mind and body to limits that I would not have thought possible 20 years ago. Family and friends thought I was crazy, and I would say, "You know, they have a club for people like me. It's called the Marathon Maniacs."

There are many amazing Marathon Maniac women (and men) who have done multiple marathons, which gives me the strength and encouragement to follow my marathon dreams. My passion for walking marathons has given me courage that I didn't know I had, the motivation to get out there every

weekend, the determination to go the marathon distance and beyond, the persistence to never give up, and the ability to stay focused. I tell people that you're never too young to start something new or to challenge yourself.

As a member of the Marathon Maniacs, I have traveled to places I had never gone before and have met some of the most amazing people across the country. And I have inspired and motivated many people on this wonderful journey. I am truly thankful that I can give back to the sport that I'm so passionate about.

Thank you, Steve, Chris, and Tony! I am who I am because of the Marathon Maniacs Club. 🐱

Good Health, Good Memories, and Great Friendships

by • David Hayes

I wasn't in track and field in high school or college. I grew too fast for my joints, so I had to sit out certain activities until I grew into my skeleton, or until it grew into me. I did row junior-varsity crew in college. Most of our training was running distance, and I outpaced nearly every other runner. I was 6 feet, 7 inches at the time and a lean 210 pounds.

When I took up running in 2006, I did it out of self-preservation. I had been an avid walker around Lake Quannapowitt in Wakefield, Massachusetts. Many Marathon Maniacs know this lake as the site for the Around the Lake 24-hour marathon, ultra, and relay. At the time, I knew of Lake Q only as a place to walk near my home, but I had always noticed that the lake was densely populated with runners. I remember being at the lake during the annual 24-hour event, never as a participant or a spectator but just as a local.

I said that I began running out of self-preservation. This is three times true. Once was a warm, humid summer night that attracted all kinds of gnats and mosquitoes. After being bitten several times, I ran to my car as quickly as I could. It may have been a quarter mile, not much more.

A particular reason why I needed to walk was that I have an inner-ear balance and hearing problem known as Meniere's disease. Since 1987, I have pursued every option available, including surgery, to mitigate the problem, but nothing helped. The problem grew worse in stages. Secondary symptoms included high blood pressure, loss of balance, vertigo, insomnia, and weight gain. These were complemented by the anxiety of having an unwelcome and permanent hindrance in my life—but walking helped.

Walking helped so much that one day (and without the encouragement of mosquitoes), I began running the grass lawns that connected the three-mile loop around the lake. Then, before I knew it, I had patched together the entire circuit until one day I ran the entire three-plus miles, my first benchmark. I remember being able to count how many times I finished the loop. Soon I couldn't remember or couldn't keep track or it just didn't matter. Next came all the standard introductions to running: sore feet because of my bargain shoes and cheap socks, shin splits, and iliotibial band pangs. These things came and went.

I tried more mileage—four-and-one-half miles, five miles, and then seven miles on one of those best-intentions treadmills that I had bought 10 years before and that had been sitting idle for 10 years, drying hanging shirts. I spent a winter running seven miles in exactly one hour every day immediately after work. I eventually wore out the motor on my treadmill. The motor just slowed down and died one day. I was very proud of this. I still am.

What followed? I lost weight, I lost most vertigo problems, my blood pressure improved, and my resting heart rate settled in at 48 beats per minute. I still had Meniere's, but now I had options. I compare how I controlled the disease to a rider taming a horse while on the horse, with the horse out of control and the rider not knowing how to ride. Just the same, the horse finally obeys and steadies over time.

Speaking of horses, I mentioned my height. I'm also a Clydesdale and once weighed 316 pounds. Today I weigh 245 pounds. I'm not lean, but I'm very strong. When I tried Chi Running, I resembled a *T. rex* and have the photos to prove it.

The second time I ran out of self-preservation was at Plum Island Nature Refuge, a beautiful barrier island in Massachusetts where I trained for my

first half-marathon. I ran into new problems, including a bloody nipple, bursa pain, and shoulder cramps, all of which I never had before. I dripped the kind of sweat that gets in your eyes and closes at least one of them.

Anyway, I was finishing this last run before my one- week taper when I was assaulted by green-head flies chewing at my legs! I was as tired as I have ever been in my life, and I found that at mile 12, I had to run full speed back to the car just to get away from the bugs.

The next week was the Boston Run to Remember half-marathon. In many ways, that training made all the difference, bugs and all, because the last two miles were highlighted by an urgent need to use the porta-potty. My brain wanted me to slow down and walk, but just as urgently it wanted me to run faster and find a toilet. In that same race, I even ran past an aid station where a volunteer handed me my first gel. I didn't know what it was so I actually turned around and ran back and gave it back to him. I laugh about that now.

I ran 1:58 at Run to Remember. This was a great moment in my life. I felt not that something had been returned to me but that something was new, a gift. I wasn't the same as before I had Meniere's, and I wasn't the same as when Meniere's had me. I think of it as a threading of humility, pride, determination, and gratitude.

Completing this half-marathon made me realize that I needed experienced running advice, so I found a great, inspiring club: the Melrose Running Club. I started to improve my running when I joined the club. I set out on the club's Sunday long-run program with great people and was able to finish the Bay State Marathon in 4:16. Since then, I've had some slower, tougher runs, like Big Sur and Valley of Fire, but I've also run both Boston and Big Sur within the same week, qualifying me as a Maniac, and at each event I posted respectable (for me) times of 4:25 and 4:27. I'm especially proud of the Big Sur finish because it came six days later and is arguably more difficult. I got to run the 50th anniversary of Mount Washington during my 50th year, and I ran a 50K on an island in Maine on one of the hottest days of the year. It was over 95 degrees, and I finished under six hours. This was where I met my first Maniacs and discovered that everyone has a story and that everyone is still adding on not just miles but memories.

As #2569, I've only recently begun to meet other Maniacs, and I like them, and as a spectator I enjoy cheering for them.

I said that I have run for self-preservation on three separate occasions. The third is every time I run. Running has generated good health, good memories, and great friendships. Now I'm trying to figure out how to get a few more Marathon Maniac stars.

Enriching Life:
Five Marathons in North America in Five Weeks

by • Anton Reiter

It is a duty for every marathon runner to participate in the famous New York City Marathon at least once. The 40th anniversary race in 2009 offered a good reason for me to do that. I had started running marathons in 2001 but stopped in 2007 and switched to triathlons. In 2008, I returned and ran the Vienna City Marathon.

Last year, at the age of 55, my passion awoke again, and I decided to travel from my home in Austria to the United States and run several marathons.

I checked *MarathonGuide.com* and started to organize my North American running tour. I decided on the following destinations: Portland (Maine); Chicago; Toronto; Washington, DC; and as a climax, the New York City Marathon. I had to plan everything in detail and had to include both the time and the financial expenditure to be expected. The Internet was my greatest aid. I arrived in New York City on September 30 by a cruise over the Atlantic. We had a rough sea but wonderful weather in New York.

On October 3, I went to Portland by car in the early morning; the ride lasted seven hours. The organizational team was extraordinarily friendly; I felt that I was in a family of runners. Some ladies even baked apple pie for the participants. Stress arose for me when checking out on the morning of race day. On a Sunday, no one was at the reception desk, so I nearly came too late to the start, which was at the university.

The Maine Marathon is hilly. I had not known this before and began too fast. My strength was all used up at 20 miles, and I was marching the rest of the distance. I finished in 4:48 and had expected a better time for my first marathon in the USA.

On the way back to New York, I made a stop in Boston to visit the city. After some days of regeneration, I traveled to Chicago. Because of its architecture and many cultural events, Chicago is a fabulous city. Probably because I was not used to the air conditioning in the hotels and the means of transportation, I received a feverish inflammation of the throat. As I felt weakened, I had to take a taxi to the marathon expo instead of taking the shuttle bus for the runners.

So I was at the start on October 10, 2009, with thick, long running trousers and a running jacket and was overwhelmed by the enthusiasm and joy that the runners showed. I was sick, but my motto was "keep up and arrive." The last two to three miles were very hard. I wanted to finish under five hours and had to mobilize all my energy to finish in 4:53. Back in the Silversmith Hotel, I took a hot bath. The next day, I felt much better and then had two beautiful days of sightseeing.

The third destination was Toronto, where the 15th GoodLife Fitness Marathon would take place on October 18, 2009. Toronto is a beautiful city. As a student in 1974, I had worked at the tobacco harvest for several weeks in Ontario (Tillsonburg) and got to know Toronto, so I was looking forward to being there. But on the day of my arrival, the wind blew a small metal particle into my right eye. I felt a lot of pain and went back to the hotel. The particle had to be taken out urgently because I could not sleep at all at night. I found a private eye clinic where I was treated efficiently. The doctor said that he had run the Toronto Marathon and was confident that I should be fit on Sunday despite my eye injury. I shared his optimism. I participated with sunglasses and thick clothes because of the cool temperatures and finished as intended, again under five hours (4:51).

Back in New York City, I did nothing but relax, eat, sightsee, and enjoy movies and tried (in vain) to get a ticket for the musical *Hair* on Broadway.

My fourth marathon destination was Washington, DC, in order to run the 34th Marine Corps Marathon on October 25, 2009. The marathon exhibition at the convention center was impressive, but unfortunately, the exclusive running gear was sold out when I arrived on Saturday.

The race started from a shut-off military ground in Arlington on Sunday. The Marines paid very precise attention that nobody except runners entered this zone. With a field of 30,000 participants, it took me 20 minutes to come to the timing mat at the very beginning of the starter's line. The course went uphill for the first five miles, but afterward, the most beautiful sights of Washington, DC, were offered to the runners. We passed close by the Pentagon and the famous Jefferson, Lincoln, and Washington Memorials. Many runners had a reference on the back of their shirt that said they were running for someone—for example, "For my beloved son who died in Iraq." It might be sadness mixed with patriotism, but it went under my skin and made me think about the sense of any war. The Marine Corps Marathon was a running celebration on a very beautiful route. I finished in 4:51 and was satisfied. After a stay of four days in Washington, I went back to New York.

The 40th New York City Marathon was the climax and the main goal of my US trip. One week before that event, Manhattan was overcrowded with runners and their families. I felt the fabulous atmosphere in Central Park when I was jogging there during the days before the race, as many others did. I was there in May 2008 and had a good conversation with the 90-year-old former running icon Alberto Arroya, whom everyone knew as the mayor of Central Park. He proudly showed me a medal from 1984, which he had received when running the New York City Marathon.

Unfortunately, the weather changed to rain. Thousands of runners got wet feet at the start because they had to wait two to three hours until the three waves started in 20-minute sequences beginning at 9:40 A.M. I was in the third wave; my starting time was after 10:20. You receive goose flesh if you inhale the atmosphere at the start.

In spite of bad weather at the beginning, the runners were in a good mood. But you should not overestimate yourself. Crossing several bridges takes its toll. And it is difficult to pass other runners as there are many thousands of us, inadvertently blocking the faster runners.

The crowd that moves forward at the start near the Verrazano-Narrows Bridge is gigantic and unforgettable. Never before had I seen so many spectators in my life. The entire route was full with applauding people standing in lines side by side; every space was filled up. You would not find such enthusiasm anywhere else in the world at marathon races.

I had a bet with a female employee of the Austrian Culture Institute that I would not lose more than 10 minutes to her. She had trained a whole year for the New York City Marathon, which was her first, while I do not train at all but consider one marathon as the best preparation for the next. She had started in the second wave and finished in 4:37. I was in the third wave and had 4:44 as a net time, which was less than 10 minutes behind her. Our results were published in the extra section of the *New York Times* the following day.

Looking back on my North American running tour, the effort expended enriched my life. I would like to become a member of the 100 Marathon Club in the coming three years. So far, I have run 63 marathons over eight years and have received many beautiful medals. To reach 100, I need to remain healthy and get no injuries.

When I retire in about six years, my goal is to become a 50-states runner, too, which means I must run a further 46 marathons in the United States.

Viktor Fankl, an Austrian neurologist, said, *Wo ein Wille ist, da ist auch ein Weg,* which means, "If you want to, you can do it."

My First Ultra and the Mental Tool Kit

by • Kelly "Mongo" Olsen

The November event began drippy and cool. All signs pointed to cool weather throughout the day, a great day for any run. The first miles were filled with a bit of self-doubt. Fifty miles would be harder than a double marathon to be sure, but how much harder? Training had gone well, and my desire (what I call, "ya gotta wanna") had me running on nervous energy early. Nonstop hills presented a day of literal ups and downs for the 12.5-mile loop course.

As advertised, the hills are unrelenting. A conversation soon begins to replay in my head with each loop: *Leaves everywhere . . . going up again . . . watch it here, a little slick . . . remember this part . . . not too wet, great . . . not too slick, nice . . . tree . . . bird . . . sky . . .* boom! *What the #$@! Why am I facedown?*

Two women running by politely ignore my swear words, and one states flatly, "You're OK; just walk it off." Everything from the waist down throbs but still seems to function. I start to walk it off as suggested, glancing back to glare at the reason for the gravity check.

The expected boulder is a small root peeking out from what two minutes ago had been a military-grade cloaking device of leaves. *Walking better now . . . systems check . . . couple of toes hurting . . . everything functioning . . . let's*

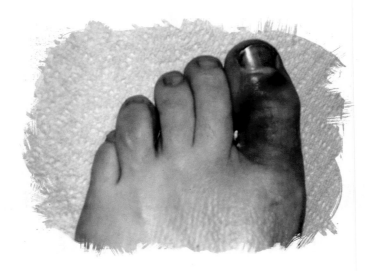

run. After a couple of miles, I give credit for the lack of pain to adrenaline, as there is now a problem with my left big toe. Seeing the smiling face of my wife, Chris, means lap three is done, and I'm looking forward to chicken soup, Advil, and dry socks for the final go-round.

I talk myself through the last loop, finishing with a strange stride, a little pain, and some satisfaction to have come within minutes of my target time.

All of you might be saying, "Broken big toes aren't a problem; everyone (except him) knows they cause only small discomfort." I prefer to think of that day as winning a mental challenge for the final 19 miles. The first ultra is uncharted territory and even on a great day is filled with uncertainty. Add injury to uncertainty, and the day quickly becomes how you deal with it.

I'm thankful to have experienced an injury in my first ultra. Now, regardless of the distance to run on a particular day, there is another tool in the mental tool kit. Sometimes desire isn't enough.

Sometimes things happen to derail your running that day. Oh, well, it happens. The trade-off is the experiences gained. Desire has a helpful companion in experience.

Postscript: *Once I finished, Chris listened to the story with a devilish grin forming on her face. Did I receive sympathy from my compassionate wife, the registered nurse? Not quite. Without realizing it, she provided me with a lesson in humility, as she took great delight over the next week photo-chronicling the rainbow of color changes of my foot for her Facebook page.*

The First Marathon
Maniac Marriage

by • Meridith Ellis

The first Marathon Maniac wedding took place in Tampa Bay, Florida, on February 26, 2006 at the Gasparilla Marathon.

Marathon Maniac #45, J. Ellis, and Marathon Maniac #100, Meridith Johnson, had been engaged for a while, and when they heard about the first Marathon Maniac reunion, they decided that would be the time to get married. The plan was for everyone in the wedding party to run the marathon and have the ceremony at the finish with all the Maniacs attending the reunion present as witnesses. The wedding party included MM #143, John Kokes, as best man. Shelby Johnson, Meridith's daughter, was maid of honor, and The Rev, MM #48, would perform the ceremony.

Everyone woke up on the morning of the marathon to what appeared to be a hurricane or tropical storm. The palm trees were bent sideways in the wind and rain—not very good weather for an outdoor wedding or a marathon! Despite the weather, Meridith, Shelby, and The Rev ran the marathon while J. and John, both injured from marathoning during 2005, walked the half-marathon.

Fortunately, the tropical storm stopped and the sun came out during the race. The bride and maid of honor ran together, with Meridith wearing a bridal veil attached to her running hat and both wearing flowery wrist corsages. During the race, Meridith and Shelby heard every possible runaway-bride joke from both runners and spectators.

Meridith crossed the finish line with arms open to her groom, who was waiting for her on the other side. The wedding party began to assemble at a tent set up just beyond the finish area, complete with wedding cake and champagne. The DJ for the race played wedding music, which surprised both runners and spectators, who were unaware that a wedding was about to take place.

While the group waited for everyone to finish the race, the Gasparilla race director came over to congratulate J. and Meridith. This was the first wedding Gasparilla had ever had at its marathon. The *Tampa Bay Tribune* was also there to record the event, which became a two-page article complete with pictures the next day.

The Rev performed a simple but very moving ceremony. It was a one-of-a-kind event that will be remembered by J. and Meridith as the perfect union of their life together as Marathon Maniacs.

J. and Meridith would like to thank the Main Maniacs for their support in allowing them to have their wedding as part of the first Marathon Maniac reunion.

66

The People's Marathon

by • Amy Yanni

I'm not a love-it-or-leave-it person, as my sense of democracy and being a responsible citizen means staying informed and always trying to improve your country. I had never thought about running the Marine Corps Marathon, as I didn't think I would fit in very well. I assumed that it was for military types and DAR/NRA members only. And it is huge, bigger than Boston, which means a whole lot of hoopla early in the morning just to get to the start line. (I prefer rolling out of bed and sauntering up with about 15 minutes to spare.)

Well, as I delicately clean the crow feathers from my keyboard, let me say this is a unique event and a race worth doing. While it is titled the Marine Corps Marathon, it is known as "the people's marathon," which evokes Marx, not marksmen. And it truly is that: a race for the people and by the Marines. That's a powerful combination.

To say that it is exceptionally well organized is redundant, and you would expect that after 32 years (this was the 33rd running) and having the Marines in charge. At the expo, I got an inkling of the unique sort of organization I am writing about here. I was finished at the packet pickup and started drifting toward the door from which I had entered when a very sharp young Marine called out: *"Ma'am! This is not an exit, ma'am! Exits are on your left, ma'am!*" with very clear arm motions to illustrate. I had never been admonished in such a respectful fashion before. Even though I was being redirected, I felt sort of honored.

Every single Marine I met made me just as proud to be an American. When so much in the news about us right now is depressing, the weekend seemed as if it were a bright oasis, with even the sun dawning for us on race day after a dreary, rainy Saturday. We gathered at the parking lot to do the usual prerace things, watch the sun come up, and begin to get a sense of how many people actually run this race. The UPS drop-bag trucks were attended by Marines—bright, friendly, urging us to have good races, and wishing us "Good luck!"

As you walk to the starting line, which is at the Pentagon, you see things that choke you up: the wheelchair athletes, many of whom are wounded veterans; person after person running with photos of comrades who were killed in action, dedicating their races to these young men and women; gray-haired vets, back again (the Marines have a term for those who have run every single MCM: ground pounders); and the petite, blonde, 20-something in a pink hoodie, with a sign attached firmly to her back that says: "proud war widow."

The prayers, the flyovers, the start of the race: it's easy to stay emotional. Then you set forth on a tour of our nation's capital that keeps your heart beating strongly. All around, you hear other languages. Many people come from other countries to run this race. It is stirring to look around and feel deeply glad that these guests are seeing a piece of America at its best, especially this year.

Marines in fatigues are at every water stop along with volunteers, and you can bet that the stops are clearly marked and usually on both sides of the street, staggered for crowd maintenance. You stop and try to thank Marines who just correct you and thank *you* for running. The course takes you past the Jefferson Memorial before entering the National Mall, where you pass numerous monuments, memorials, and landmarks: the Lincoln, FDR, Korean War, and Vietnam Veterans memorials; the Washington Monument; and the US Capitol. Now you're about to head back toward Virginia for the last 10K—tired, sure, but you are part of something that manages to transcend the ordinary confines of a marathon on an autumn Sunday. You've had time to reflect upon what it means to be an American.

You have been reminded of whatever pieces of our nation's history are important to you as you pass by various buildings, streets, and monuments. You consider elections as you pass the White House and the history we are making right now—all the people who stood up for and too many who had to die for the ideals that make us a free country, people dedicated to achieving equal access to justice for everyone. You keep going, and the crowds keep exhorting you to stay the course.

You do and are greeted by a row of Marine Corps lieutenants, standing straight and tall and holding finisher's medals in their hands. One of them is for you. As soon as it is draped on your shoulders, along with the Mylar blanket, someone guides you over to the Iwo Jima Memorial so that a photographer can snap your picture in front of it. Then you head on out to walk out the kinks and continue contemplating what just happened.

You know, I never thought I would run this one. After signing up, I figured that it would be good to do it once. Now I can't wait to go back.

Voted "best marathon for families," the Marine Corps Marathon continues a tradition of dedication, sportsmanship, and patriotism. Runners from all walks of life have participated in the world's largest marathon that doesn't offer prize money, deservingly earning the nickname "the people's marathon."

I Went Running Outside

by • Jakob Herrmann

There I was, standing on the scale in spring 2005, not too happy, thinking that I'm just 3 pounds away from reaching 200. I hadn't done any kind of sports whatsoever since high school, which was over 20 years ago. *I've got to do something; I've got to lose some weight,* I thought. So I started to run on treadmills.

I hated treadmills with a passion, but a particular event in April 2005 changed everything. On that day, I once again forced myself to go for a run in the little gym of my apartment complex. After a few minutes, one of the air conditioners broke and the whole room filled with a burning-rubber smell. I didn't want to stop my exercise, so I tried something new: I went running outside.

And I instantly loved it.

I loved it so much that I ran a half-marathon just six weeks after my first step outside the gym. And 21 days later, I ran my second half-marathon. And just 33 days later, on the first October weekend in 2005, I crossed the finish line of my first full marathon. I had caught the running bug. I wanted to do more and go farther.

That wish came true in November. I didn't bother trying out a 50K first but directly jumped into a 50-miler: the JFK 50. I crossed the finish line with a huge smile 12 hours, 7 minutes, and 49 seconds after the start. I was happy, but I felt a burn inside me for more.

I then tried a 100-miler. I chose the 2006 Rio del Lago 100 because of its "easy" course and the fact that it was close to where I lived. Although I was nervous, I was able to successfully finish that race.

That first 100-miler sparked a bunch of other races and other great challenges. I'm proud to say that I've done 86 races so far in the past five and a half years including nine half-marathons, 36 marathons, 11 31-milers, eight 50-milers, two 62-milers, and nine 100-milers. The biggest challenge so far has been running the Angeles Crest 100, the Disneyland Half-Marathon, and the Rio del Lago 100 in only two weeks in 2010.

And yes, I've lost 40 pounds so far, thanks to running.

The Youngest Maniac

by • Scott Spangler

In November 2009, I made my goal of joining the Marathon Maniacs by running two marathons in two days. At the time, my 11-year-old-son, Steele, had seen his uncle wearing a Maniac shirt at smaller races, and once I joined, he told me that he wanted to as well.

The week before New Year's, he told me that his goal for 2010 was to qualify for the Maniacs. I had seen how much he loved running, and he had already run two half-marathons, each in two hours or less, plus he had run in 185-plus-mile relays in consecutive years so I thought he might be capable of running a marathon but wasn't sure about qualifying.

We ran the New Year's marathon in Bothell, Washington. He ran with me the whole way and although tired, he told me that he was glad he did it. He also told me that he didn't want to run another one for a couple of years, so I said that's fine and just figured that it would be a few years before he accomplished his goal of qualifying for the Maniacs.

About two months later, we got a call from King 5 News (in Seattle) asking to interview Steele for a story. All of a sudden, Steele wanted to run another marathon so he could be on television. The story was filmed on May 21, and on May 22, he ran his second marathon, again at Bothell. I loved running with him.

I was scheduled to run the Green River Marathon on June 5. As we drove home from that second marathon, Steele was thinking pretty hard and asked whether he would qualify as a Maniac if he ran that marathon with me. The race was within 16 days, so I told him that he would. He asked if he could run it, and I said that we would see how he felt. After a couple of days, he still wanted to and wasn't sore, so I signed him up.

He was very excited on the day of the race. He kept telling people that he was qualifying that day, and he was noticed by a few people who had run the other marathons with him as well as those who had seen him on the news. He had a great run and was happy to finish. As soon as I got home, I registered him for the Maniacs, and he was officially number 2600. He told his friends at school, and he said that it was a great feeling to have accomplished that goal.

What I remember most about it is that he said he enjoyed it most of all because he got to run it with me. Every parent wants to hear that.

What an awesome kid he is, and I know he represents the Maniacs well, even at the age of 11.

Our Palladium Project

by • Carlos Hideaki Fujinaga

Many people say that a marathon can change your life. Trading experiences with people who have the same passion can open many new horizons.

When I was a college student, I had a disease in my spine and needed a cane to walk. I think the pain that I felt to walk even just one kilometer then cultivated some power in me to run marathons for fun without any suffering now.

Fortunately, I recovered without surgery. After two long years of Oriental Seitai therapy (like chiropractic) as a sedentary fat boy, I wanted to enjoy my happiness of walking with my legs only (without the cane). I needed to choose one sport to practice.

My father was an elite runner in his youth (he held the Brazilian youth record for 3,000 meters in 1964 (9:04). He inspired me. Three months after I restarted walking, I completed the traditional São Silvestre International Race, walking almost all the 15 kilometers. One and a half years later, I ran my first marathon, the Rio de Janeiro Marathon. The next year, 2008, Rodolfo Lucena, the first and the only Brazilian Maniac at that time, told me about the Marathon Maniacs.

I then ran a marathon in Santiago, Chile, my first marathon in my hometown São Paulo, and another marathon, again in Rio de Janeiro. From this, I got my first star and number 1024 and became the second Brazilian Maniac. In the same year, I met Nilson Lima and invited him to join the group. Three months later, I identified João Gabbardo at the Curitiba Marathon with his yellow singlet. It was the beginning of a big project.

The next year, 2009, saw an increase in the number of Brazilian Maniacs. João, Nilson, and I ran all six official Brazilian marathons and other marathons in South America, inviting or meeting other runners to make the Marathon Maniac journey with us.

During that year, João told us about his great dream when he will be 55 years old: he wants to go to the United States and run 55 marathons in 2011. My running friends and I wanted to move to a higher level in the Marathon Maniacs—to go from Iridium to Palladium. As there is no opportunity to run many marathons in a short amount of time in Brazil, we decided to travel to the United States to run the needed races, and we called the trip "The Palladium Project."

During the project, we visited places like New Orleans, the Grand Canyon, and Key West. In total, we visited 25 states.

We rented a car. One time, João drove from Philadelphia to Los Angeles and from Los Angeles to Orlando in two weeks and ran six marathons. Another time, Nilson and I went from Orlando to Wisconsin and back to Miami, running four marathons. It was a wonderful experience!

If I can say something in English (despite some mistakes), it is because of the Marathon Maniacs. Although I had English classes at high school, I am more confident in my ability to speak English now because of my contacts with Marc Frommer (MM #9), the Main Maniacs, and all the Maniacs I was pleased to meet.

I just need to go to Washington now.

I Became a Marathon Addict

by • Rodrigo Damasceno

I'm from Brazil and started to run 10 years ago, in 2000, when I was 16. I decided to start training for the fourth Rio de Janeiro Half-Marathon. The race occurred one day after my 17th birthday. The second race occurred two years later. Running wasn't yet an addiction, but I decided to run a marathon. My first marathon was in 2003, in Rio de Janeiro, where I live. It was my fifth race. My idea was just to finish. My second marathon was in 2008, during my senior year at university.

In 2009, I decided to run two marathons in 30 days, one in São Paulo and another in Rio de Janeiro. A friend said to me: "If you do another marathon in the next 60 days, you can become a Marathon Maniac." I found the third one in Santa Catarina. It was a trail marathon. That was my goal: do three marathons and become a Marathon Maniac.

After that, I decided to do as many marathons as possible. In 2009, I found two more in Brazil, but I realized that if I would like to do more than 10 in a year, I would have to go outside Brazil.

My first non-Brazilian marathon was the 2010 Disney Marathon. But the big trip truly started in February, one week after Carnival—Rio de Janeiro's world-famous festival, which is held before Lent every year. I decided to stay two months in Europe and run nine marathons.

I started in Barcelona, doing my best time ever (4:09), and then I did the Rome Marathon. But the most difficult challenge in this trip was to finish the Jurassic Coast Challenge, in England, which was three trail marathons in three days. After that, I did marathons in Paris, Vienna, St. Just, and Stratford-upon-Avon (the last two in England).

I did one more marathon one week later in São Paulo after I got back to Brazil. It was May, and I did one more trail marathon in Santa Catarina before the end of the month.

Now it's July, and in a couple of days I'm going to do my fourth Rio de Janeiro Marathon.

I became a marathon addict. Now it's a pleasure to start a trip just to do a marathon. It's impossible now to go abroad without running a marathon. I have now run 19 marathons, 14 after I became a Marathon Maniac, in less than a year. At this moment, I'm a ruthenium Maniac! 🐱

The Brohawk Was Born

by • Jawn Angus

Not sure if this brief story is worthy of adding to your book, but I thought it fell under the category of weird and wacky, so I figured I would share.

Maniac #112 (Terry Sentinella) called me in early 2009 and talked me into registering to run the Chicago Marathon with him in October. After I agreed to run it with him, I stated that I was trying to get faster and that I was doing speed work. He told me that we should get Mohawks for the race, as they would be more aerodynamic and I would run faster. Of course, that sounded like a logical idea to me! I trimmed only the sides and back of my head for the next five months.

Come October, the brohawk was born! I chose purple for my Mohawk, and Terry chose red. I ran a 13-minute PR at the time, and Terry qualified for Boston!

Dashing Through the Snow

by • Ashley Kuhlmann

"This is one of the craziest things I have ever done," I told fellow Marathon Maniac #660 (Andy Fritz) as we headed out in 17-degree weather and 2 to 3 inches of snow. We were going to run our first 50K, which I thought was insane enough in itself, but running it in winter-wonderland conditions amped up the insanity. In preparation, I donned two layers of clothes on the bottom and four layers on top with additional hand warmers stuffed in my pockets and gloves. Even with all the layers, I was still cold while we waited for the race to start.

We set out in darkness with 20 other diehard runners. Running into the sunrise glittering on the snow was gorgeous, but I soon realized that running in snow has its challenges. The footing was uneven due to footprints frozen in the snow, so with every step, minor adjustments had to be made. With every footfall, there was a tendency to slip backward, hindering forward propulsion. The longer we ran, the more challenging it became. About an hour into the run, I realized that my gels had frozen solid and had to thaw them out by sticking them next to my hand warmers. Icicle formation in eyelashes and hair made you look a little crazy but also made it hard to blink. Eyelashes stuck together!

The halfway turnaround was a welcoming sight. Maniac #660 and I both took a little hot chocolate, and then it was back to the crunching of snow. The second half of the race, we started taking more walking breaks. I had to will my legs to run again after each one. The sun was dipping into the west as we neared the finish. It had been a long day, and seeing that finish line was one of the greatest feelings. Not only had I just run farther than ever before in my life, I ran it in abnormal conditions and with a fellow Maniac. Pigtails Flat Ass 50K would be a race that I always remember.

It was during that race that I had my defining moment. I realized that being a Marathon Maniac means that you run for the love and joy of running and sharing running with others. We had no time goal or pace chart. We were just happy to be out there running. It is the same whenever I run with another Maniac or spot one during a race. There is a sense of camaraderie and understanding. At the root of it, we are all a bit crazy, and we are all out there doing something together that we love.

Here's a short running poem that captures this love.

My toenail fell off
the sacrifice I have to pay
for my running

Estes Park Marathon

by • David England

I believe that it takes three things to be a long-distance runner: time, money, and good genes. I have none of these in sufficient quantities. Yet I continue to challenge my schedule, our bank account, and my body just to experience the camaraderie, the endorphins, and the pure satisfaction of beating myself up with a bunch of other Maniacs (club members or not) for 26.2 miles.

Oh, and I almost forgot, the fourth thing that it takes is the ability to think that you are *the smartest person on the planet.* This means that you do not have to worry about things like proper training, such as when you live and train at sea level and then try to run a marathon at altitude. This is what I attempted on June 15, 2008, at the Estes Park Marathon in Colorado.

The Estes Park Marathon has a low point of around 7,420 feet above sea level and a high point of 8,150 feet above sea level. My thinking was that this should not be a big deal for someone with 23 previous marathons; after all, I am the smartest person on the planet and do not need to listen to anyone's advice. Hey, after all, isn't it completely meaningless that America's Olympic athletes train at Colorado Springs, which is about 6,000 feet above sea level? Remember, as I mentioned, I am the smartest person on the planet.

My wife and I arrived in Estes Park two days before the run. We found that we had difficulty sleeping, a few headaches, and some lack of appetite, but hey, these are not symptoms of altitude sickness. Nah! It's just jet lag and travel discomfort, nothing to worry about at all.

Sunday morning arrives, and the excitement of the run has built into its usual heart-pounding chaos. I've had very little sleep, too many bathroom trips, not enough coffee, and lots of warm juice and burnt toast. Many statements of "Hey, where's my water bottle and gels?" and "Seen my hat anywhere?" Nip guards are on, and Bodyglide is applied. "What's the weather like?" Sunblock on. "Hey, check the time. We've got to get to the start!"

Heather, my wife, navigates us the four or so miles from our rented cabin to the start of the race at the Estes Park Middle School complex. We're standing around with the crowd, 15 or so minutes before the race was to start, doing the usual prerace things—talking, stretching, pacing, and wishing I didn't have to pee again—when it suddenly hits me. Where are my water bottle and gels?

"Oh, my god! I never do a marathon without them! I can't go the whole race without my gels and water bottle!"

It seems that in the race-morning haste, I left them on the counter in the cabin. (Remember that I said that I am the smartest person on the planet.) OK, it's now seven or so minutes to the start. Heather graciously suggests that she will drive back to the cabin, find the elusive bottle and gels, and deliver them to me somewhere on the course since she isn't running.

What a perfect plan!

A newfound friend I was talking to in the group has a suggestion. If I jog around to the back of the gymnasium (a distance of about 100 yards), I may be able to find some hangers-on at the expo. They may be able to provide me with a gel or an energy bar to get me through the first few miles.

Another perfect plan!

I kiss Heather adieu, she leaves, and I merrily jog off around the back of the gymnasium. About 20 steps into my jog, I suddenly find that my vision starts to narrow and I can't breathe normally. I'm gasping and sputtering. Tears are beginning to well up in my eyes, and my legs refuse to move. My brain screams *WTF*, and I then realize that I am in serious trouble! I suddenly get it. Within a millisecond, I understand: altitude, yes, altitude. I should have known. After all, I am the smartest person on the planet, but who would have thought that it would affect me?

I stop. By now, I can see the doors to the gymnasium. They are closed, and I realize that no one is there. *OK, recompose,* I boldly say to myself and stride off, slowly, toward the start of the race. I have two things going for me: (1) I've done 23 of these runs before (at that time), so I should know what they're all about; and (2) I am the smartest person on the planet!

I make it to the starting area with about three minutes to go before the start, just enough time to realize that I now have to pee really, really badly! There isn't enough time to worry about that, though, as I have a much graver problem to contend with: where can I find some oxygen?

The gun fires, and we're off!

I won't bore you with the infinitesimal details of the race; they are far too revealing and embarrassingly painful to relate, but it went something like this:

- **Mile one**—surprisingly, feeling not too bad

- **Mile five**—starting to get my stride

- **Mile 10**—lack of oxygen starting to be an issue, slowing considerably

- **Mile 15**—lack of oxygen is an issue, slowing even more dramatically

- **Mile 20**—lack of oxygen is a problem, walking now

- **Mile 25**—there is no oxygen in Colorado, walking very, very slowly! My feet are dragging, and occasionally I'm gulping for oxygen. Hey, is this the fabled Wall?

- **Mile 26.2**—Made it; 5 hours, 29 minutes, and 28 seconds! A personal worst! But I'm alive!

So here are some words of wisdom from the smartest person on the planet. When someone has something to tell you about a specific race, such as, "Boy, was that one hilly!" or "You know, that race is over a mile high," it's probably worth thinking about how to adjust your training and, maybe more important, your attitude.

So now, with 40 of these runs completed, have I listened to my own advice? Nah! Why bother? After all, I am the smartest person on the planet.

74

The Gift

by • Cheri Fiorucci

The marathon is a gift. It's one we cherish and one that we wonder why we accept in the first place. Either way you look at the gift, it is one that teaches you the most about yourself. Today was such a day.

As I was standing at the start, the temperature was toying with us. The cloudless blue sky promised hot temperatures. There I stood in a sea of marathoners, lost in my own thoughts and in complete anticipation. My first marathon in a year, and my nerves were getting the best of me.

The horn blasted. It had begun. We ran through the city's center before passing the farmers' market on our way up the first hill, taking us away from the oceanfront and into the country roads. The rural landscape was beautiful and brought rolling hills. Each hill that we crested delivered a feeling of accomplishment and renewed determination. I felt good. I felt strong. If I could maintain this pace, I would reach a personal record.

That was mile 10. How quickly a race can turn.

By mile 12, the heat was getting to me. Shade became sparse, and the sun was merciless. I hit the halfway point and just couldn't run up another hill. I had to walk. Despite my disappointment, I could not—would not—lose the run this early. Having been down that self-beating-up road before, I had no desire to revisit it. My goal became to finish. As hard as it was, I let go of the PR that I had felt was achievable a few miles earlier.

Despite the rural roads, the course was incredibly well supported. Aid stations were heard before they were seen. Loved ones of other marathoners were seen several times along the course. I adopted these families, and they began shouting encouragement to me as I passed by.

At mile 19, a woman turned to me and said, "What were we thinking?" I laughed while introducing myself. A mom of four, Susan was running her first marathon. We passed time talking about everything and nothing. The two of us, complete strangers hours before, became instant best friends. Pain and agony do that. It's part of the gift. You connect with people that you would never have connected to before. Our backgrounds were diverse, but here we were, pulling each other through the same moment in time.

Mile 24 began a descent toward the finish line. After crossing the finish line, I collapsed into my husband's arms and wept. I was spent. The clock confirmed my worst marathon time, but it didn't matter. It was the most challenging course I had run and the biggest gift that I could give myself. Susan crossed the finish line smiling amidst tears. Hugging me, she told me that she couldn't have done it without my encouragement. I told her that I felt the exact same way.

The gift is not found in the finisher's shirt or the medal hanging around your neck. The gift is found in learning about yourself. In 26.2 miles, you dig deep within yourself to rise above the conditions and the doubt that comes with exhaustion. Crossing the finish line, you find out you are pretty darn tough and can take whatever life can give. The gift is learning what you are made of.

In three weeks, I will do it all over again, and I wonder what the gift will bring that day.

Kountry Mart
Invades
Kansas Again:
"Ultra Mart"

by • Steve Grady

After a disappointing DNF at Rocky Raccoon in February 2009, I was determined to finish my first 50-miler, the Heartland 50 in Cassoday, Kansas. Part of my training during the summer of 2009 included the Hog's Hunt 50K in Huntsville, Texas, in May and the El Scorcho 50K in Fort Worth in July. I included back-to-back long runs on most weekends during the summer as well. To make sure that I had a reasonable chance of finishing my first 50-miler, I decided to run/walk the Patriots' Run in Olathe, Kansas, on September 11. This would serve as my last long run before the Heartland 50.

This training adventure began in "country-mart" style. After I met fellow Marathon Maniac Johnny "the Animal" Spriggs in Broken Arrow, Oklahoma, we traveled through the farmland of northeastern Oklahoma, Missouri, and Kansas to the Patriots' Run. Runners complete three-quarter-mile loops on an asphalt trail until 9:11 P.M. This is run every year to remember the brave Americans who lost their lives on 9-11-2001. This run also honors our brave men and women serving in the armed forces.

Johnny and I arrived in Olathe 20 minutes before the start. We picked up our race packets and proceeded to construct peanut butter and jelly sandwiches on the tailgate of a Toyota pickup truck. These sandwiches would serve as our lunch and for carbohydrate snacks during the run. We gulped down a sandwich, drank some cola, and then proceeded to run!

It was near 85 degrees at the noon start and during the afternoon. I suffered quite a bit during the first 27 miles. Johnny drove to the local store after he finished his 26.2 miles to obtain some cool ones. He consumed these beverages while sitting on the tailgate of the pickup. He cheered me on every lap. As he consumed these spirited beverages, Johnny motivated me by saying, "You have at least 15 more laps in you." Finally, the sun went down and it cooled off. I started to feel really good. Before you know it, my watch read 9:06 P.M.

I finished my last lap at 9:11 P.M., right on the dot! I was thrilled to find out that I had just completed 40.756 miles. I told Johnny, "I reckon I'm ready for the Heartland 50 now!" I'll drink to that!

Well, it had been a month since the Patriots' Run and time for another trip to good old Kansas. So I turned up the bluegrass music, and my wife and I headed up Interstate 35 through Okieland to big "K" country once more! Cyndi reluctantly put up with the bluegrass music for a few hours. Finally, we reached our destination: Cassoday, Kansas, the prairie chicken capital of America! I obtained my race packet, and then we all consumed vast quantities of Kansas vittles. We had roast beef, mashed potatoes, cream gravy, Texas-sized dinner rolls, salad, and cake. The vittles were great! Festus on *Gunsmoke* would say, "These vittles are doggone larapin good!"

My wife and I then proceeded south on the Kansas Turnpike to our race hotel. After a good night's rest, Cyndi and I woke up at 4 A.M. and then proceeded 20 miles up the turnpike to Cassoday. Finally, it was time for the 6 A.M. start. The ultrarunners lined up in the pitch dark. I knew I was in Kountry Mart heaven as you could hear the hound dogs bark and howl! This was a motivating start for me.

The scenery was breathtaking as the sun rose. I ran the flats and walked the hills in the beautiful prairie! These were *big* hills, too! Don't ever think that all of Kansas is flat. The Flint Hills of Kansas near Cassoday are rolling hills and prairie. It was a bit cool and windy (35 degrees with 35- to 40-mph winds). But I lived in Kansas in the early 1980s, so I knew what was in store for me. I stayed within my running capabilities and ate well at the aid stations. This was the best run of my life, and I intended to enjoy every bit of it!

There were only two houses along the way and no human spectators. There were many Black Angus cattle along the way. In my mind, they were cheering me on, telling me to keep moving! I saw one black snake with orange stripes lying on the gravel road at mile 35. He looked none too happy in that 35-degree air! I didn't bother to consult with him. He probably had already kicked the bucket, anyway.

Before you know it, the Cassoday water tower was in sight! I was getting close and could see Cyndi in the distance! I knew that my father and mother were both watching from above! They had passed on a few years ago but were there in spirit. As I crossed the finish in 11 hours, 54 minutes, I could hear cheering and race director Jim Davis ringing the cattle bells. This was a country-mart dream come true. "K" for Kansas! "K" for Kountry Mart!

Life Is What We Make of It

by • Rosemarie Jeanpierre

I've been overweight most of my life. I was 9 years old when I started gaining weight to the point of obesity. In the Philippines where I grew up, it is very uncommon for kids to be overweight. I stood out because I was the "fat girl" and so, naturally, I was the center of ridicule. School was really traumatizing for me. Every day was a nightmare. My classmates bullied me and made fun of me. Kids can be cruel. I remember when the boys would poke me with a safety pin thinking that I would deflate like a balloon. They would also pull the chair I was sitting on so I would drop on the floor. They were always trying to humiliate me. I developed an inferiority complex. I didn't have any confidence to speak up. I was suppressing my emotions, which probably led to the intense migraines I was having.

This went on from elementary all throughout high school. I felt alone and isolated from the rest because of the way I looked. Food was the only comfort that I had. I wouldn't stop eating. I loved food too much—the way it made me feel was not something that I was willing to give up. Even though I hated myself for it, I still tried to fill in that emotional gap within me through food. Even my parents couldn't stop me. I was sickened by what I saw in the mirror, but I felt that it was who I was and that I couldn't do anything about it. I had fallen in the pit of depression. I was ashamed of myself. I wasn't living up to my potential. I knew that there had to be something more in life than my endless shame of being overweight.

I needed to do something about the way I looked. My first attempt to lose weight was at the age of 20, but it was very unhealthy. I starved myself and exercised too much. I lost around 50 pounds from 185. And then I got married and moved to the United States. I was longing for my family back home, and I used food to stuff my feelings and to fill the days that I was homesick. I gained all the weight that I had lost and started to get heavier and heavier. It was like I was always hungry. Without making any conscious decisions about my food intake, I would just eat food I craved, such as hamburgers, fries, shakes, ice cream, and chocolates.

Heart disease and diabetes run in my family. My father passed away because of a heart attack. My weight problem had been bothering me so much that I started suffering from joint pain, fatigue, and severe migraines. At the age of 39, I made up my mind to do something about my health. One trip to the doctor confirmed one of my greatest fears. I knew that my unhealthy lifestyle was not without consequence. I was diagnosed with hypertension, a prediabetic medical condition, and out-of-range cholesterol levels and was high risk for coronary heart disease.

It was at that moment that I realized that I had to choose to be healthy and change the way I lived. At first, it was hard to step out of my comfort zone and face this challenge. But I was determined. I researched all about fitness and nutrition, reading books and magazines to educate myself about the right way to gain a healthy lifestyle. To paraphrase Maya Angelou, "The more you know, the better you do." Knowledge is power. I knew what I had to do.

I started going to the gym (cardio and weights) and eating healthily. My daily food consumption before I started was between 6,000 and 7,000 calories of greasy fried food, sweets, bread, and rice. Now my daily food intake is about 1,500 to 1,800 calories, high in protein and low in fat and carbs. I eat lots of fruits and vegetables, baked chicken or tuna, wheat bread, and no added sugar. Even though there were some people who thought that I couldn't do it, I persevered.

When I lost half of my weight and began running marathons, I was in the top shape of my life! I never dreamed that I was capable of doing it. Somewhere along the way, I realized that I was really good at it. I started competing and winning medals. Who could have known that I would become an athlete? All my life, I've been searching for something to ignite the passion in me. I've finally found it in running. It

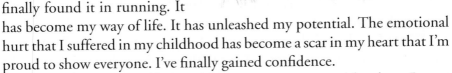

has become my way of life. It has unleashed my potential. The emotional hurt that I suffered in my childhood has become a scar in my heart that I'm proud to show everyone. I've finally gained confidence.

And now I'm compelled to share my success story with others. I want to help people who are going through what I went through. I want to give them inspiration and make them realize that life is what we make of it. We're all capable of improving ourselves and achieving our goals in life with perseverance, determination, faith, and support from family and friends.

Opening Our Eyes

by • Phillip Fields

As an average marathoner, I ran 3:30s in the 1980s, 1990s, and 2000s. I qualified for Boston in 1996 with a 3:25 and in 2004 with 3:35. In January 2007, a tuneup marathon suggested that I was ready to attempt to qualify for Boston again. However, four weeks later, I noticed an alarming change in my stamina. I couldn't complete three miles without walking. Following eight months of cardiovascular, respiratory, and gastrointestinal exams, the doctors had no clue. At my yearly checkup that September, my physician discovered enlarged lymph nodes and a high white blood cell count. I was referred to the Mitchell Cancer Institute in Mobile, Alabama. Further blood tests, a bone-marrow biopsy, and a second opinion confirmed chronic lymphocytic leukemia.

When I explained the importance of running to my oncologists and asked about running marathons, I was told that taking the trash out would be fatiguing, much less running a marathon. And besides, I would likely be starting chemotherapy within six months.

After a year of twice-a-day training to learn to run with the fatigue, I decided to attempt a marathon in February 2009 in Pensacola, Florida. The race start was my scariest moment ever. In training runs, I was hitting The Wall at six miles and would force myself to do 10 more. However, 20 more miles was an unknown. The marathon was two loops. Passing the half-marathon finish and continuing the second loop totally out of gas was mental. However, I figured I wouldn't get closer to finishing a marathon, and if I quit, would I ever again be able to force myself to complete one? Although I was not close to qualifying for Boston, I was elated with my time of 4:30 and began planning my next marathon. At Little Rock in March 2009, I heard about the 50 States Marathon Club and set a goal of running marathons in all 50 states and DC with leukemia.

In a way, leukemia has been a blessing. Because of the fatigue, I'm not running marathons as fast as I would like, but I am having a blast going from state to state and seeing our great country while doing what I enjoy—running marathons. I would never have done this without leukemia.

My favorite marathons to date are Choteau, Montana (afterward, I hiked Glacier National Park); Sedona, Arizona (afterward, I stayed at El Tovar on the rim of the Grand Canyon); and South Dakota, which started at the Crazy Horse Monument near Mount Rushmore. The hardest was Estes Park, Colorado, because of its altitude. I guess that having sufficient red blood cells really is important.

As a Christian, I believe that things sometimes happen that are designed to open our eyes. We have to be ever vigilant for when that happens and seize the moment, or else it will pass you by and you will continue to be lost.

My moment came at the Prairie Fire Marathon in Wichita, Kansas, in October 2010. The race director contacted me about having the local newspaper do an article about my running marathons around the country with leukemia. From 2007 to 2010, I had kept my leukemia known to close friends only but figured that since no one knew me in Kansas, what the heck. A lady in Wichita read the article, tracked down where I was staying in Wichita for the marathon, and called me. She said that she was inspired and encouraged by what I had accomplished. She went on to tell me about her young daughter, who had recently been diagnosed with leukemia and was starting chemotherapy. Her story touched me, and I knew what I had to do.

I began to research foundations that focused on the treatment of childhood diseases, especially cancer. I read volumes of information on the National Leukemia Society and St. Jude Children's Research Hospital and all the good work they were doing. I checked out how much of the donations coming in were spent on treatment rather than administrative costs and advertising. I then learned about a foundation that devotes all its time and resources to the research and treatment of childhood diseases, especially cancer. The foundation is Nemours.

I developed a website (*www.marathonwithleukemia.org*) that went online in January 2011. With the help of Nemours, I have begun raising money for the treatment of children with cancer. Now when I go places, articles are published in local papers, and I have the website and "Running for Kids With Cancer" printed on my running shirts. Foundations like Nemours are dependent on donations. The National Cancer Society budgets $4.8 billion a year to cancer research. Less than 4 percent, about $175 million, is devoted to pediatric cancer. That is why the newest treatment for children's leukemia was developed nearly 20 years ago.

On the website, I have attempted to show viewers photos of all the places I have traveled. That way, even if they go to the website out of curiosity and don't donate, at least they will come away with a sense of how great our country is.

Running appeared to delay my need for chemotherapy; however, in February my oncologist informed me that it was time. Again, my question to the oncologist was whether I could continue to run during chemo. His response this time was, "Do whatever you feel like doing. However, you are not going to feel like doing much." Since there were no states where I hadn't run a February marathon, I ran the Mardi Gras Half-Marathon in New Orleans on February 13 and the Five Points of Life Half-Marathon in Gainesville, Florida, on February 20. These were one and two weeks past the first round of chemotherapy and were my attempts to see whether I would be able to run a marathon in Maryland after the second round of chemo.

The Run Crazy Horse Marathon race director, Jerry Dunn, finished his e-mails with, "Don't limit your challenges . . . challenge your limits, and have fun doin' it." I guess that is what I have been doing. In May 2011, Boise, Idaho, will be the 32nd state where I have run a marathon with leukemia in 28 months and my third during chemotherapy. Believe me, it is easier taking the trash out.

I can't begin to stress to people how important an exercise program is to improve your quality of life as you age. Chemotherapy is not for sissies. My treatment was on three consecutive days every 21 days. In spite of seven different antinausea prescriptions, the three days would be followed by three days of not being able to keep anything but Popsicles down. At the end of this period, I would be an average of 13 pounds lighter and require a fluid IV. Two weekends later, I would be running a marathon and get back in time for the next treatment. I know elderly and frail people who didn't survive the first round of chemo. Being in shape definitely helped me get through this.

I was asked what I would do when I completed all 50 states. I answered that I would start over, since there are lots more places to visit in each state.

Contributors

Christine Adams (story 2) is a case manager for a preschool program for low-income kids in Washington State. Christine started running to lose weight. She has reached her goal weight and continues to be active in running, Zumba, and hot yoga.

Gary Allen (story 10) has run most of his life on a small offshore Maine island where the main road is only two miles long. He estimates that he has covered around 75,000 miles on that single piece of broken road. "Running out on Great Cranberry Island made me at times feel like a caged lion, and when I got out into the world to run a race, it felt easy simply because I felt free."

Malcolm Anderson has written three books on marathon running: *The Messengers*, *A Marathon Odyssey*, and *The Cayman Island Marathon Experience*. He is the host of a television show called "26.2 and Beyond: A Marathon Journey," which follows the training of several runners as they prepare for marathons and ultras. Malcolm has run over 40 marathons and ultras, including the 90K Comrades ultramarathon in South Africa, the Tahoe Triple, and the Brathay 10 marathons in 10 days Challenge in the Lake District in England. His most important event was a 5K Wolfe Island race, which he ran with his sons, Callum and Jack, in 2008. He has his sights set on running longer distances, including more trail running, and at least one 100-miler! He lives on a small farm in southeastern Ontario, Canada, somewhere near the middle of nowhere. You can read more on Malcolm and his writing at *runplaces.com*.

Jawn "Marathawn Jawn" Angus (story 71) lives in Seattle and is a planner in the petrochemical industry. He joined the Marathon Maniacs in part because he travels for work, so he's always in new places meeting new people. "It's good to always see familiar faces at marathon races no matter what city I'm in."

Joe "Moonie" Arcilla (story 15) figured that running would be the last thing he would enjoy in his quest to forever lose his excess weight nearly a decade ago, but after losing 140 pounds, that very same running has become a bit of a passion. He once thought that qualifying for the Marathon Maniacs in the manner he did might be something of an ultimate accomplishment, but that was trumped in 2010 when he finally found that proverbial soul mate (and fellow runner to boot.) Both of them look forward to making many trips, marathon distance and otherwise, well into the future.

Barefoot Jon (story 18) has been a minimalist runner since 1977. Jon's barefooting started on a whim in 1990 when temperatures soared to 97 degrees for the Goodwill

Games Marathon in Seattle. His "barefootness" now includes ultras from 50K to 112 miles as well as cycling two all-barefoot Ironman events. When necessary, his favored footwear is flip-flop thongs. But for fun, as a member of the Japan 100-Marathon Joyful Running Club, he has run in Japanese wooden geta and waraji straw sandals, jika-tabi rubber construction shoes, cloth zori, and tabi socks.

Mike Brandt's (story 28) "extremophile" running adventures (100-plus marathons) have taken him around the world. He has run on the Great Wall of China, in Antarctica, past the moais on Easter Island, on the Inca Trail, through the streets of London, past the Sea of Galilee, on the Tibetan Plateau, and to the tip of South Africa. He has run marathons and climbed mountains on all seven contents.

Ken Briggs (story 16) is the CEO of Spokane Valley Partners. Ken also teaches at Whitworth University and has been in management in the nonprofit sector for over 28 years both in Seattle and Spokane, Washington. Ken ran track (the half mile) in high school and college in San Francisco. He lives with his wife of 38 years and two aged cats.

Pamela Brulotte (story 48) lives in Leavenworth, Washington, with her husband of 17 years and three children. She runs when she can in between helping run the businesses that she and her husband started (Munchen Haus Bavarian Grill & Beer Garden and Icicle Brewing Company) and spending time with her family.

Stephen Bucken (story 54), age 21, is an industrial engineering student at the University of Florida. He has run eight marathons, including his first ultramarathon in 2011. He has also competed in three Ironman 70.3s, including the world championships in Las Vegas in 2011. His father, Klaus Bucken, has gone on to run four marathons and recently broke the four-hour mark. "Running continues to keep us very close, and neither of us plans on stopping any time soon."

Caroline Burnet (story 7) began her running career when she was recruited by a persistent high school cross-country coach. Never speedy, she has since compensated with distance and found in the Marathon Maniacs a group that thankfully supports such an approach. When not logging therapeutic miles or sidelined by overuse injuries, Caroline works as a project manager at an architectural firm in Atlanta, Georgia.

Claire Carder (story 20) has been a runner all her life; she graduated from high school before Title IX or surely would have competed in track. She has been a Maniac since 2009, the year she discovered that she "really loves long runs." The running life, as well as living in the beautiful city of Portland, Oregon, she says, "has kept me fit and sane."

As first a middle-of-the-pack and now a bottom-third finisher, **Rodney Chang** (story 51) still enjoys participating in 26.2s as an "Average Joe." At 66, he motivates himself by photographing courses, making art of the best shots, and documenting the routes on his website *MarathonCoursePhotos.com*.

In 1993, **Moses Christian** (story 43) began training for his first marathon, which he completed at the age of 61. He has now done 168 full marathons and 37 unofficial marathons. In this time, he also survived prostate cancer. At the age of 79, he is still going strong, running and working full time in his surgery practice. His passions include charity work in an orphanage and a medical clinic in India. He runs marathons now with his son, Rajan Christian, who has done 46 marathons.

Elizabeth "Tiggie" Culver (story 9) has been a runner for 14 years. She had run many shorter distances when she decided to run a marathon before her 50th birthday, and she completed it in Austin, Texas. She began her journey to become a Maniac with friends Kim "Eeyore" Heimbecker and Rick "Pooh" (with an "h"!) Deaver in the inaugural San Antonio Rock 'n' Roll marathon in 2009. They became Maniacs together when they finished Marathon #6, Big D Texas, in April 2010. They still run together today!

Rodrigo Damasceno (story 70) is from Rio de Janeiro, Brazil. He became a Maniac in 2009 when he did three marathons in Brazil and three in the United States. In 2010 he started running international marathons. He did one in the United States and nine in eight weeks in Europe. As of November 2011, he had completed 28 marathons and some ultras. "And I'm still training for my next challenges," he reports.

Cheri Damitio (story 56) enjoys running on trails and logging roads near her home in the Coast Range in western Oregon. She loves meeting fellow runners and giving and getting encouragement from other Maniacs in marathons. Someday, when she grows up, she dreams of running a BQ.

Paul C. David (story 27) lives in the Seattle area with his triathlete wife, Kris Solem, and their two daughters. When not out on the trails, he is a software engineer and loves photography and reading. Today looks like a good day for a run.

Rick "Pooh" Deaver (story 9) always wanted to run a marathon before turning 40 (did not happen) . . . OK, before 50. He signed up for his first marathon at 52. He ran San Antonio Rock 'n' Roll in 2008 and decided that he would not run a marathon again. Eight weeks later, he ran his second marathon. Rick started training and running with friends to run three marathons in three months to become Maniacs. "I could not have done it without my running buds—Kim "Eeyore" Heimbecker and Lyz "Tiggie" Culver."

Bob and Lenore Dolphin (stories 13 and 42), commonly known as "Team Dolphin," are fondly known as the world's oldest marathon race directors. At the age of 70, they started working on the Yakima River Canyon Marathon in central Washington State. The inaugural race was held on March 31, 2001, and they are looking forward to their 12th annual YRCM on March 31, 2012. Bob's first marathon was the Heart of America Marathon in Columbia, Missouri, which he ran at the age of 51. Ten years later, he ran his 100th marathon at the same race. He is planning to run number 500 at their YRCM. Lenore, who has volunteered in hundreds of marathons, is not a runner but supports Bob's running. Team Dolphin was inducted into the Maniacs' Hall of Fame on March 27, 2009. In March 2001, they were asked by Peter Graham of the United Kingdom 100 Marathon Club to start a club in North America. Since then the club has grown to over 300 members. Bob is the first American member of the original UK club and is also a member of the German and Japanese 100 Marathon Clubs.

Meridith Ellis (story 65) works in accounting. To keep harmony in the family, she became a Marathon Maniac and discovered the insanity of back-to-back marathons. Running and walking continue to be a huge part of her life. **J. Ellis** is a service manager for Kenworth Northwest. He started running in the Marines and stopped immediately upon discharge. Five years later, he started running again to lose weight. He moved up to running marathons and began doing back-to-back marathons in different states before the Maniacs became a club. When Marathon Maniacs was formed he "had to be" a member.

David England (story 73) lives in Richmond, BC, Canada. He shares his life with his wife, lover, and best friend Heather and their two cats. When he's not running, golfing, gardening, or doing never-ending home improvement projects, he can be found working for Velcro Americas as an account manager. He joined the Marathon Maniacs in 2002 and became Maniac #281 during a brief moment of sanity when it occurred to him that he needed to address his long-distance running addiction. He advises that there is no cure—just solace in camaraderie.

Ed "Mad Hatter-Fancy Pants" Ettinghausen (story 60) ran his first five marathons at the age of 17 and 18. He then took a 28-year break for college, marriage, kids, and work! He rediscovered the pure joy of the marathon world in March 2009. Since then, Ed has completed 166 marathons and 36 ultramarathons, joining a certain club of like-minded marathon wackos in June 2009. Shortly after the 2010 Boston 2 Big Sur marathon Ed-venture with Bob Dolphin, Ed dropped the support boot and replaced it with a jester's costume.

Phillip Fields (story 77) is a professor of anatomy at the University of South Alabama. Diagnosed with leukemia in 2007, he has been on a quest since 2009 to complete a marathon in all 50 states. He became a Maniac after seeing people wearing Maniac shirts at various marathons. He is raising money for Nemours, a foundation that specializes in research and treatment of pediatric problems, especially pediatric cancer.

Cheri Fiorucci (story 74) Cheri resides in Lynden, Washington, with her husband, Dennis, and their sons Stefan and Dane. "How appropriate that the sanity of my long runs brought me here, home to the Insane Asylum, with my fellow Maniacs."

Carlos Hideaki Fujinaga (story 69) lives in Sao Paulo, Brazil. He runs a tour company that specializes in sports. Rodolfo Lucena, the first Brazilian Maniac, challenged Carlos to complete three marathons in three months, and since then he has run in several marathons around the world. His greatest experience so far has been a two-month visit to the United States, which he spent running marathons and meeting Maniacs.

Linda Garbo (story 50) is an RRCA-certified running coach, a certified personal-fitness trainer, and owner of Artemis Fitness. Linda is a lifelong runner, new to the marathon distance at age 55. She finds that combining her 29 years in education, her own personal fitness, and her belief in keeping people healthy and active are a great combination for coaching.

Perky Garcia (story 46) was originally a competitive bodybuilder and started running to cut weight. She discovered that the longer she ran, the more calories she burned, and she found the perfect balance between calories in versus calories out. Beth Davenport told her about the Maniacs and she finally found her people. "We are nestled gently between the Hash House Harriers and Boston Qualifiers!"

Known as "the medal guy," **Paul Gentry** (story 49) runs seven or eight marathons each year and plans to finish number 50 in 2013. In addition to being a Maniac, he is also a Half-Fanatic and a Brooks ID PACE team member. Paul writes for *Marathon & Beyond* each year and has written music heard on the radio around the world.

David Hayes (story 62), age 51, is "not just a Clydesdale, but at 6 feet, 7 inches and 255 pounds, I'm a Percheron." He is a programmer and graphics developer with BNY Mellon Asset Servicing. When not running, he likes snowshoeing, back-country skiing, fly-fishing, and yoga. He would like to run a marathon or play bocce ball on an oil supertanker.

The year 2010 was an exciting one for **Yolanda Holder** (story 61). She now holds four titles: the *Guinness World Records* holder of "Most Marathons Run in a Calendar Year" by a woman (106 marathons in 2010); Marathon Maniac of the Year 2010; Pacific Coast Trail Champion 2010 (age group); and Trail Blazer Champion 2010 (age group). "A special thank you to Steve, Chris, and Tony for founding this amazing club."

Megan Ross Hope (story 26) is a spiritual director in Seattle, Washington. At age 9, she ran her first 12K and has been addicted to running ever since. Now with seven marathons completed and a lot of life ahead, Megan is always looking for new running challenges and is willing to travel the world to find them. To learn more about neurofibromatosis, please visit the Children's Tumor Foundation website, *www.ctf.org*.

Tom Hosner (story 52) lives in Southern California. He joined the Maniacs in 2007, two months before completing his 100th marathon or ultra at the San Diego Rock 'n' Roll Marathon. He is now approaching 200 races. He has introduced marathoning to many coworkers and friends and even his two daughters, who ran their first marathon at Dad's 100th. It was a special day for Tom.

Kristine M. Jahn (story 17) is a mom, a wife, a runner, a vice president, and someone who can't pass up a challenge. Having lived much of her childhood and early adulthood as a morbidly obese individual, she found the inner strength and motivation to make a lasting lifestyle change.

Rosemarie Jeanpierre (story 76) used to be morbidly obese and was diagnosed with related diseases such as prediabetic condition and hypertension and was at high risk for coronary artery disease. Through good faith, discipline, determination, support from family and friends, and passion for running, she lost half of her body weight, dropping from 220 to 110 pounds. She adopted a healthy lifestyle and became a Maniac in 2009. She believes the club is a great way to promote fitness and health.

Brian Joachims (story 19) lives in Norman, Oklahoma, with his wife, Michelle; they have two children, Christine and David. Brian has been cycling recently but continues to run marathons and half-marathons and is also a member of the Half-Fanatics.

David H. Johnson (story 55) joined the Maniacs in April 2009. While David was running the Cowtown Marathon, another runner said, "You need to join those nuts." David is director of Running Preacher Ministries, a nonprofit organization based in Texas, which uses his running to raise awareness and donations for various needs. He also speaks to groups of all ages on staying active and helping others. David and his wife, Deborah, have two children and two granddaughters who give him his greatest, but most enjoyable, endurance challenges.

Don Kienz (The Rev) (story 11) lives in Pennsylvania and has officiated at one wedding of two Marathon Maniacs after completing three seminary degrees and 72 marathons . . . which reflect his faster road to peace with the infinite versus his infinite times falling to pieces on the roads. The Rev enjoys maniacism despite his lack of ability and appreciates the founders' welcome and their keeping it fun. He reflects on members' experiences in a monthly column in the Maniac newsletters. The Rev has been married for 34 years to Mrs. Rev, Pamela Cole, and is the delighted dad of three sons who golf.

Ashley Kuhlmann (story 72) lives in Lakewood, Washington, and works as a dietitian. She learned about the Marathon Maniacs five years ago while running her second marathon (the Tacoma City Marathon), when she had "the pleasure of running with a pack of them." Over 26 miles, they convinced her that she should join the group, and now she says, "Here I am, 52 marathons (and counting) later."

Mike Kuhlmann (story 34) was 56 when he started running. He ran his first marathon in 2007. He has now run 85 races, including 60 marathons and ultramarathons. He and his wife have five children, three of whom are also Marathon Maniacs. He and his children recently ran a 200-mile relay race as an ultra team. His wife does not run but enjoys the running stories.

Paige Kurtz (story 45) was always "the girl picked last," avoiding all sports involving throwing or catching for her own safety. When she realized that "left foot, right foot, repeat" was safe and that she could keep doing this for a very long time, she became a marathoner. Paige also helps people regain functional use of their hands and arms, working as a certified hand therapist and occupational therapist.

Robert López (story 30) (aka "Stevie Ray," aka "McLovin") is an old-school Maniac from Seattle. A refugee from the IT world and sometimes a corporate trainer, Robert has completed over 300 marathons across all 50 states in less than 10 years. His favorite race is the Kona Marathon. His heroes are Terry Fox and Larry Macon. Besides running, he loves puppies, pie, beer, Hawai'i, and writing. Robert runs because he likes to travel to new places; running gives him an excuse to do so.

Ed Loy (story 8) is based in Honolulu. He started running to lose weight and get in shape. After finishing his first half-marathon and full marathon in 2007, he thought the marathon thing was super hard and the distance was crazy long. He became a Maniac in 2009. His long-term goals are to complete the 50 states and to run in Europe as well.

Rodolfo Lucena (story 36), 54, is a Brazilian journalist and blogger who loves to run around the world. He was a couch potato until the late age of 42, when he ran his first marathon, got hooked, and ended up becoming the first Marathon Maniac in Latin America (#370). He has written two books about running. Rodolfo lives in São Paulo, Brazil, with his lovely wife, Eleonora, his two wonderful daughters, and some dogs.

Danny Lyon (story 58), best-selling author of *The Colour of My Underwear Is Blue*, is married to Connie Lyon and is the father of three teenagers, Tommy, Davey, and Maggie, all living in Alberta, Canada. After losing 64 pounds when he was 17, Danny began running and has found ways to enter races, first while travelling throughout the United States and overseas as a telecommunications technician for 20 years and then, in the last 15 years, as a business owner, author, and speaker.

Dave Major (story 22) continues to breathe life into his running by always setting new targets and challenges. "I get the most satisfaction seeing sedentary friends and colleagues take up this global sport, whether for recreation or fitness improvement or to compete." He feels "positively enriched" in helping people achieve the same level of satisfaction and pleasure from their running that he has been so fortunate to experience. "Look after your running, and it will look after you, too, and most importantly, enjoy it!"

Linda Major (story 22) started running because she was told by doctors that she couldn't run. With help, advice, and perseverance Linda managed to complete her first race in April 2000, a local 10-miler. She then wanted to complete a marathon but was again told she couldn't. Six years later, she completed her 100th marathon and five years later her 300th. "No one tells me I can't do anything anymore! Until you try, you just don't know what you are capable of. Even if you try something once and don't like it, you have achieved something."

Letty Marino (story 57) is a network systems administrator in Virginia. Letty started running while in the Navy and hated it. She got out of the Navy after 10 years while going through a divorce and ran to relieve stress. She liked the way it made her feel, so she ran more. She is now married to a wonderful man who fully supports her running; he has even joined her in a few marathons. Letty has two older boys, both of whom have served in the Marine Corps and have told her they will *never* run a marathon because running was all they ever did in the Marines. Recently, Letty and her husband adopted a little boy, Nicolas, who loves to run races. Her husband feels Letty has "corrupted" Nicholas. At a recent 5K, the organizers gave all the little kids who ran a Beanie Baby, and his response was, "I don't want this. Where's my medal?"

Marci Martin (story 3), age 46, has completed eight marathons so far. In addition to three children, she and Bob have a minidachshund named Bullseye. During the work week, Marci is a special-education teacher. They live in Hoquiam, Washington. Marci is looking forward to running many more marathons. **Bob Martin**, age 55, has so far completed 38 marathons and one ultramarathon. He has been married to Marci Martin for 28 years. They have two grown sons and a daughter. During the working week, Bob is a truck driver.

Brandon Mead (story 59) is a 25-year-old Texan who received an honorable discharge from the Army in 2009. He lives in Longview, Washington, with his wife, Katie Mead, and attends Washington State University Vancouver, where he is studying environmental science. He joined the Marathon Maniacs in October 2010.

Pam Medhurst (story 47) started running 32 years ago and found that she wasn't very fast, just really consistent! Pam has done over 250 marathons, several triathlons, double-century bike rides, ultras, half-marathons, and a number of mud runs over the years and has achieved two black belts. It all started from that first run around the block that she wrote about. She is also a volunteer search-and-rescue canine handler with the local sheriff's department.

Valerie Merges (story 39) is a hospital pharmacist in Utah. She works evening shifts so she can run in the morning before work (or snowboard in the winter). She longs for the day that she can quit her job and write about her adventures full time. Valerie lives in Utah so she can compete in triathlons during the hot summer months and spend the winters snowboarding. She became a Maniac in 2009 after meeting a friendly group of people who asked, "What number are you?" prior to a back-to-back marathon event.

Mike Moore (story 38) became a Marathon Maniac in 2010. He entered medical school after working as a physician's assistant in surgery, critical care, and emergency medicine. He has worked in information technology and as a helicopter pilot. During his U.S. Army service, he qualified as an airborne ranger. He is married and has two children. He is a global medical-student blogger for the *TheLancetStudent.com* and is a frequent guest on *The Marathon Show* (*www.themarathonshow.com/*).

Craig Newport (story 12) lives with his wife in Orangevale, California. He traces his interest in running marathons to reading a book about the history of the Boston Marathon. He accidentally qualified to be a Marathon Maniac before the club was formed.

Kelly Olsen (story 64) is "Mongo" on race day, a Maniac since 2008, and a self-aware running addict. While he currently lives in New England with his wife and two daughters—the three most understanding people and best runner support on the planet!—his occupation has caused them to live and work in several U.S. states and foreign countries, often relocating just ahead of running interventions planned by folks "trying to help."

Cami Ostman (story 6) is the author of *Second Wind: One Woman's Midlife Quest to Run Seven Marathons on Seven Continents*. She is a licensed marriage and family therapist with publications in her field. Cami has been featured in several publications, including the *Mudgee Guardian* in Australia, *The Bellingham Herald* and *Adventures Northwest* in Washington State, *La Prensa* in Chile, and, most recently, *Fitness* magazine (November 2010) and *O, The Oprah Magazine* (January 2011). She completed her seventh marathon on a different continent by running in Antarctica in March 2010. Cami lives in Bellingham, Washington.

Ingrid Peterson (story 32) is a retired physical therapist who started running in 2007 with the Leukemia & Lymphoma Society's Team In Training. She has been involved in 12 marathon events with the group, raising more than $30,000 and still going strong. Along the way, she has run 30 other marathons so she can continue to eat ice cream.

In 2003, **Tony Phillippi** (story 1) cofounded the Marathon Maniacs with buddies Steve Yee and Chris Warren and still plays an active role in the day-to-day operations of the business. It all began on that fateful day after the Coeur d'Alene Marathon when a friend, Terry Watanabe, called Steve, Chris, and Tony a bunch of "Marathon Maniacs" at the Moon Time Tavern. Then, with the help of Mark Ariyoshi, they all began creating the trademark logo, the website, and the criteria for the club. Tony, dedicated to his love of running, partnered with Fleet Feet Sports buddy Paul (Sawdust) Morrison to create the Tacoma City Marathon Association (TCMA) in 2006. The TCMA now puts on six events, including the Michelob Ultra Tacoma City Marathon, and also manages several charity events throughout the year. Also during 2006, Tony was brought together with Databar, INC, and together they formed the company Databar Events. Tony's current goal is to someday have a faster marathon time than his Main Maniac partners, but for now he will settle for having the biggest biceps!

Maria Poranski (story 45) is a special-education teacher in Virginia; she started a running club at her school and loves sharing the joy of running with the children. Prior to registering for a marathon through a charity, her only running experience was chasing the ice cream truck when she managed to find a quarter just as the truck slowly passed her house. She can be found in the back of the pack, taking pictures and smiling her way to the finish line.

Beth Ramirez (story 4) began running six years ago. She believes that running keeps her sane and healthy and out of trouble. A Southern California native, Ramirez also enjoys traveling, hanging out at the beach, and playing golf with her husband.

George Rehmet (story 41) is a special-education teacher for community schools in San Mateo County, California. He started running in 1981 and became a Maniac in 2009. He is looking forward to being the first person to have swum to or from Alcatraz 100 times (completed) and to have run 100 marathons (he is two-thirds of the way).

Anton Reiter (story 63) lives and works in Vienna, Austria. He has been a secondary academic-school teacher, a lecturer for multimedia didactics and media philosophy at universities, and a head of a department at the Austrian Ministry of Education and Science. He is married and has a 21-year-old daughter who is studying law and who ran the Vienna City Marathon at the age of 14 in 3:25.

Valentine-John Ridao (story 37) is a bible student and teacher by vocation and a health information management specialist by avocation. He retired from the USAF in 1991 and began ministry. Val finished his first marathon at age 53. He married Regina in December 2007 in Hawaii, one week after finishing the Honolulu Marathon. His 89-year-old dad was his best man! At Val's present pace, he hopes to qualify for Boston in 2053.

Diana Ringquist (story 5) is an overstretched mom of two, an Army wife, a professor at two universities, a private business owner, a Girl Scout leader/volunteer community coordinator/trainer/ whatever-else-needs-doing-for-the-girls, a community volunteer, an ardent supporter of anything in which her husband is involved, and a photographer. She started running at age 38 after she retired as chief operations officer of a medical conglomerate. Her goal was to run a "whole, entire mile." Diana is a proud member of the Maniacs and has run 11 marathons, innumerable half-marathons and other distances, and one triathlon in which she broke both arms but finished the race anyway. The basis of her personal philosophy is, "Find a way, make a way."

Jason Rogers (story 33) lives in Smyrna, Georgia, and works in environmental protection. He completed his first marathon in March 2009 and is now immersed in the world of trail ultrarunning.

Dean Schuster (story 40) writes about the running subculture at *www.zerotoboston. com*. He was duped into running on promises that it was an "inexpensive" sport. When not running, Dean is a partner in a mobile- and web-usability consultancy called true-matter, a job he has never successfully explained to his mother. When not complaining about a chronic groin injury, Dean enjoys fund-raising for his next adventure, the Antarctica Marathon (*www.runningwithpenguins.com*).

Bhasker Sharma (story 31) lives in Bangalore, India, and works as a senior manager at Alcatel-Lucent India, a telecom company. He recently cofounded a company called Running Buddy Sports Private Limited to help improve the experience of runners in India by providing services and products such as training and coaching, running footwear, and accessories. Bhasker was intrigued and motivated when he discovered the Marathon Maniacs website in early 2007. He set a goal to qualify as a member by the end of that year. He's now completed 27 marathons and five ultramarathons. His thoughts and experiences with running are recorded at *http://maniac808.blogspot.com*.

Peggy Shashy (story 29) is a veterinarian and avid bird-watcher who lives in Jacksonville, Florida. She started running in 2001 and ran the Gate River Run, a 15K race, for her 40th birthday. Her training partner decided that they should run the Disney marathon the following January. She runs five days a week. She and her boyfriend are trying to run all 50 states and see as many national parks in each state as possible.

Rob Roy Smith (story 35) is an attorney in Seattle, Washington, who enjoys running from the law. Rob became a Maniac in 2007 and has dragged his wife, Susannah, across the United States and the Atlantic for marathons.

Scott Spangler (story 68) lives in Port Orchard, Washington. He's an account executive for a fire alarm company in Seattle. A father of nine children, he says he is lucky enough to have a wife and one of his sons who are also Marathon Maniacs. He decided to become a Maniac because it seemed a little crazy to run two marathons in two days and because it made him smile when people told him he was crazy for doing it. "It is the most positive group of people around, and I love being associated with them all."

Dave and Vicki Stout (story 21) live and run in Bainbridge Island, Washington. They like to say, "If you live long enough, you will find a club to belong to." The Maniacs are their tribe!

Kelsey Swift (story 14) is currently pregnant with her third child and taking a break from running. She plans on getting back into it in the future.

Chris Warren (story 1) is one of the three founding members of the Marathon Maniacs (Maniac #2) and lives in Washington State. Chris ran his first marathon at the 2000 Seattle Marathon and has currently run 192 marathons in 34 U.S. states and six countries. He has also completed 15 ultramarathons. In 2008, Chris ran 53 marathons in 52 weeks, pushing him to the highest level within the club (10 stars). In 2012, he will run his 10th consecutive Boston Marathon and hopes to continue that streak as long as he can continue to qualify for the race. Chris's best time in the marathon came in 2010 (age 42) at the Napa Valley Marathon, where he ran 2:49:56. He hopes to complete the remainder of the 50 states within the next five years. For the first eight years of the club, while working a full-time job, Chris managed the inventory and shipped out all of the Maniac gear that was ordered by members.

Marsha White (story 25) is a 64-year-old librarian, copyeditor, and indexer who began power walking just 4 1/2 years ago. Since then, she has completed a marathon in all 50 states and (so far) a total of 90 marathons or ultramarathons. She plans to do marathons in the Canadian provinces and several European countries. Her dream is to walk across Great Britain north to south and east to west.

Kim Williamson (story 23) lives in Oregon and started running in March 2006. By October 2006, she completed her first marathon. Kim qualified as a Maniac after completing the Disney World Goofy's Race and a Half Challenge in 2008 and two weeks later the Miami Marathon. She is a breast cancer survivor and in her spare time loves playing with her dog, a pit bull/boxer mix named Lucy, and volunteers her time to help animals.

Steve Wisner (story 53) has been a Maniac since 2008. A runner all of his life, he took a 25-plus-year break from marathons before returning to the distance in his hometown of Olympia, Washington, at the Capital City Marathon in 2006. Steve is a graduate of Washington State University and is a hotel general manager with Hilton Hotels in San Diego.

Barb Wnek (story 44) is a physical education and health teacher for kindergarten to sixth grade in the Ferguson-Florissant School District near St. Louis, Missouri. She also teaches physical education for the Gifted Resource Council's Summer Academies. Barb completed her quest to run a marathon in every state in December 2010 at Kiawah Island, South Carolina. She ran her 100th marathon at the Pasadena Marathon in May 2011 and is a member of the 100 Marathon Club.

After 25-plus years as a public-interest lawyer, **Amy Yanni** (story 66) joined Teach For America and is teaching first grade in Hazlehurst, Mississippi. The demands have caused Amy to cut back to running very early in the morning, before school, and just three miles or so. Marathoning was great conditioning for keeping up with 6- and 7-year-olds!

Steven Yee (story 1), also known as the Maniac Prez or MM #1, started his running career in 1983. Six months later, he ran his first marathon (Tacoma, Washington). Since that fateful day, he has been hooked on the 26.2-mile distance. He has run about 260 marathons (give or take 10) and has run marathons in China, Australia, Germany, Ireland, the Netherlands, and Canada. Steve says it seems like it's taking him forever to finish the 50 states (currently at 45), but he intends to complete the task within the next few years. A 10-star Titanium Maniac by virtue of running 57 marathons in 2005, he knows that his best years are behind him, and his yearly goal is to get a Boston qualifier. His personal best was achieved 20 years ago at the Twin Cities Marathon (2:49:58), and he has a few personal-worst times over the six-hour range. Nowadays, he follows far behind in the footsteps of his Maniac founding partners Chris Warren (MM #2) and Tony Phillippi (MM #3). These two are his "roll" models! When he isn't busy running or performing Maniac duties, he works as a process analyst at a wastewater-treatment facility, where his favorite slogan is, "It's the smell of money!" He is also proud to add that he influenced a few of his coworkers into joining the "Insane Asylum"; three other Marathon Maniacs work in the same building as the prez.

Marie Zornes (story 24) began running in 2003 and ran her first marathon in 2005. She had a great time and knew that she wanted to run another. Marie heard about the Marathon Maniacs a few months after she ran her marathon. She thought it was the craziest thing she had ever heard. By 2007, she was a Maniac. When she is not running marathons, she enjoys spending time with her family, walking their dog, and traveling (especially if a marathon is involved). She is currently a full-time nurse and goes to school full time.

Marathon
A
N
Insane
Asylum
Criteria

To become a member of the Marathon Maniacs, you need to complete one of the following criteria. Whichever streak you complete will determine your placement within the level.

Bronze Level ★

1. Two marathons within a 16-day time frame.
2. Three marathons within a 90-day time frame.

Silver Level ★★

1. Three marathons within a 16-day time frame.
2. Six marathons in six consecutive calendar months.
3. Eight to 11 marathons within 365 days.

Gold Level ★★★

1. Four marathons within 37 days.
2. 12 to 18 marathons within 365 days.
3. Four marathons in four different US states, countries, or Canadian provinces (any combination) in 51 days.

Iridium Level ★★★★

1. Four marathons in 23 days.
2. 19 to 25 marathons within 365 days.
3. Two marathons in two days (or 48 hours). Must finish both races!
4. Nine marathons in nine different US states, countries, or Canadian provinces (any combination) within 365 days.

continued

Ruthenium Level ★★★★★

1. Three marathons within three days.
2. 26 to 30 marathons within 365 days.
3. Four marathons within nine days.
4. Three marathons in three different US states, countries, or Canadian provinces (any combination) within a 10-day time span.
5. 13 marathons in 13 different US states, countries, or Canadian provinces (any combination) within 365 days.

Osmium Level ★★★★★★

1. 31 to 37 marathons within 365 days.
2. 16 marathons in 16 different US states, countries, or Canadian provinces (any combination) within 365 days.
3. Six marathons within 16 days. With proper planning and rest, this can be done!
4. Four marathons in four days = Quadzilla.

Palladium Level ★★★★★★★

1. 38 to 44 marathons within 365 days.
2. 20 marathons in 20 different US states, countries, or Canadian provinces (any combination) within 365 days.
3. 13 marathons within 79 days.

Platinum Level ★★★★★★★★

1. 45 to 51 marathons within 365 days.
2. 23 marathons in 23 different US states, countries, or Canadian provinces (any combination) within 365 days.
3. 28 marathons within 183 days.

Titanium Level ★★★★★★★★★

1. 52 or more marathons within 365 days.
2. 30 marathons in 30 different US states, countries, or Canadian provinces (any combination) within 365 days.
3. 20 countries within 365 days.